Volume **15** # THE GOLDEN BOOK ENCYCLOPEDIA

porcupine to Rocky Mountains

por-roc

An exciting, up-to-date encyclopedia in 20 fact-filled, entertaining volumes

Especially designed as a first encyclopedia for today's grade-school children

More than 2,500 full-color photographs and illustrations

GOLDEN ®

From the Publishers of Golden® Books

Western Publishing Company, Inc.
Racine, Wisconsin 53404

ILLUSTRATION CREDITS
(t=top, b=bottom, c=center, l=left, r=right)

1 l, Michael O'Reilly/Joseph, Mindlin & Mulvey Inc.; 1 r, Tom Powers/Joseph, Mindlin & Mulvey Inc.; 3 bl, E. Hanumantha Rao/Photo Researchers; 3 br, Frank Mayo; 4 br, Tomas D.W. Friedmann/Photo Researchers; 5 br, U.S. Postal Service; 7, John Rice/Joseph, Mindlin & Mulvey Inc.; 8, Pat Caulfield/Photo Researchers; 9 bl, Brad Hamann; 9 cr, Lloyd P. Birmingham; 10, AP/Wide World; 13 and 15, Marcus Hamilton; 16 br, David Lindroth Inc.; 17, A. Schoenfeld/Photo Researchers; 18 tl, Lloyd P. Birmingham; 18–19 b, Tom Powers/Joseph, Mindlin & Mulvey Inc.; 20, Roger A. Clark, Jr./Photo Researchers; 21, Brad Hamann; 22–23 t, Joel Snyder/Publishers' Graphics; 23 b, Dan McCoy/Rainbow; 24, Michael O'Reilly/Joseph, Mindlin & Mulvey; 25 tr, Lloyd P. Birmingham; 26 tl, Manfred Kage/Peter Arnold, Inc.; 26 tr, Biophoto Associates/Photo Researchers; 27, Manfred Kage/Peter Arnold, Inc.; 28 tr, Petit Format/A. Gout/Photo Researchers; 28 bl, Suzanne Szasz/Photo Researchers; 29 t, Ginger Chih/Peter Arnold, Inc.; 29 bl, Hank Morgan/Photo Researchers; 30 both, Porterfield/Chickering/Photo Researchers; 32, Dennis O'Brien/Joseph, Mindlin & Mulvey; 33, © 1980 Henson Associates, Inc.; 34 and 35 bl, Brad Hamann; 35 t, reprinted with permission from *Creative Classroom*, copyright © 1987 Macmillan Educational Company, a division of Macmillan, Inc.; 36, David Rickman/Publishers' Graphics; 38, Porterfield/Chickering/Photo Researchers; 39 br, Science Photo Library/Photo Researchers; 40, David Lindroth Inc.; 41, Edna Douthat/Photo Researchers; 42 bl, Bruce Roberts/Photo Researchers; 42 br, William Strode/Woodfin Camp; 44 tl, Tom McHugh/Photo Researchers; 44 tr, Phil A. Dotson/Photo Researchers; 45, Dick Luria/Photo Researchers; 46–47, Michael O'Reilly/Joseph, Mindlin & Mulvey Inc.; 48 inset, courtesy National Radio Astronomy Observatory/Associated Universities, Inc.; 49, Bettmann Archive; 50 t, Amtrak; 50–51 b, Tom Powers/Joseph, Mindlin & Mulvey Inc.; 51 t, D. and J. Heaton/Stock, Boston; 52, Dennis O'Brien/Joseph, Mindlin & Mulvey Inc.; 53 t, Gary Ladd/Science Source/Photo Researchers; 53 inset, Dennis O'Brien/Joseph, Mindlin & Mulvey Inc.; 54 bl, Brian Brake/Photo Researchers; 54 br, Tom McHugh/Photo Researchers; 56 b, Timothy Eagan/Woodfin Camp; 56 inset, Joe Munroe/Photo Researchers; 57, Scala/Art Resource; 58, Fiona Reid/Melissa Turk & The Artist Network; 59, Mary Anne Fackelman-Miner/The White House; 60, Mei- Ku Huang, M.D./Evelyne Johnson Associates; 61 tl, David Lindroth Inc.; 61 br, Jeff Myers/Photo Researchers; 62, Jerry Jones/Photo Researchers; 63, Culver Pictures; 64, Tom Powers/Joseph, Mindlin & Mulvey Inc.; 65 br and 66 b, Scala/Art Resource; 66 inset, Bettmann Archive; 67, National Gallery of Art, Washington D.C., Chester Dale Collection; 68 tl, Biophoto Associates/Photo Researchers; 68 tr, Kenneth W. Fink/Photo Researchers; 69 tr, Biophoto Associates/Science Source/Photo Researchers; 69 bl, John Rice/Joseph, Mindlin & Mulvey Inc.; 70 bl, R. Andrew Odum/Peter Arnold, Inc.; 71 bl, Robert Frank/Melissa Turk & The Artist Network; 72, Michael O'Reilly/Joseph, Mindlin & Mulvey Inc.; 73, David Rickman/Publishers' Graphics; 74 tl, Bettmann Archive; 74 tr, Culver Pictures; 75, Courtesy of The Valley Forge Historical Society; 76 tr, David Lindroth Inc.; 76–77 b, Giraudon/Art Resource; 77 tr, S. Nagendra/Photo Researchers; 79 tr, Marilyn Bass; 79 br, Eunice Harris/Photo Researchers; 81 b, Tom Burnside/Photo Researchers; 81 inset, Lloyd P. Birmingham; 82, Nicholas Devore III/Bruce Coleman Inc.; 83 tl, David Lindroth Inc.; 83 tr, John Rice/Joseph, Mindlin & Mulvey Inc.; 84, © Joe Viesti; 85 t, Walter H. Hodge/Peter Arnold, Inc.; 85 b, Edna Douthat/Photo Researchers; 86 tr, Bettmann Archive; 86 cl, Marilyn Bass; 87 tr, UPI/Bettmann Newsphotos; 87 br, Hank Morgan/Photo Researchers; 88 t, Dan McCoy/Rainbow; 88 inset, Lowell Georgia/Science Source/Photo Researchers; 89, Charles R. Belinky/Photo Researchers; 91, NASA; 92, Tom Powers/Joseph, Mindlin & Mulvey Inc.; 93, Harrison Funk/Retna; 94 tl, Trainor/Photo Trends; 94 tr, Henry Grossman/Transworld Feature Syndicate Inc.; 95 b, Kent and Donna Dannen/Photo Researchers; 96, Nicholas Devore III/Bruce Coleman Inc.

COVER CREDITS
Center: Manfred Kage/Peter Arnold, Inc. Clockwise from top: Tom McHugh/Photo Researchers; © 1980 Henson Associates, Inc.; Michael O'Reilly/Joseph, Mindlin & Mulvey Inc.; Phil A. Dotson/Photo Researchers; Lowell Georgia/Science Source/Photo Researchers; Edna Douthat/Photo Researchers.

Library of Congress Catalog Card Number: 87-82741
ISBN: 0-307-70115-8

ABCDEFGHIJK

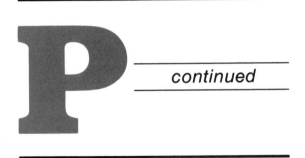

continued

America. They climb trees and they do not burrow.

The *North American porcupine*—a New World porcupine—is usually about 60 centimeters (2 feet) long. It is a good swimmer and climber. When threatened, it raises its quills, turns its back on the enemy, and attacks by rushing backward! The quills of North American porcupines have *barbs*—sharp hooks at the tips. When these quills enter an enemy's skin, they cannot be removed without tearing the skin.

See also **rodent.**

porcupine

The porcupine is a large rodent, related to rats and mice. Its coat includes many long, sharp spines called *quills.* When the porcupine is angry or afraid, the quills stand up straight, like pins in a pincushion. If an enemy touches the quills, they come off and become stuck in the enemy's skin. The porcupine then grows new ones.

Porcupines spend the daytime between rocks, under bushes, or in burrows in the ground. They come out at night to feed on bark, buds, and plants.

There are two kinds of porcupines—Old World and New World. Old World porcupines live in Europe, Africa, and Asia. They stay on the ground and nest in burrows. New World porcupines live in North America and South

pork

Pork is the meat of a hog. It is sold in various *cuts*—pieces such as chops or roasts. Pork ribs are usually cooked with a sauce and barbecued.

Ham is a pork cut taken from the back leg or shoulder. Bacon comes from the back or sides. Before being sold, ham and bacon cuts are covered with a sweet liquid. This process, called *curing,* helps the meat last longer without spoiling. It also adds flavor.

Like most meats, pork is rich in B vitamins. Pork is also a source of *protein*—an energy-supplying substance that helps build and repair the human body.

If a porcupine is attacked, it turns its back and ruffles up its quills.

Different cuts of pork come from different parts of the pig.

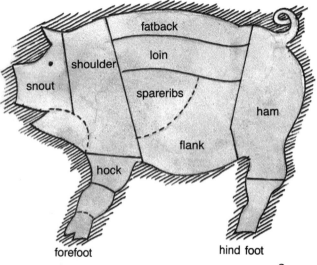

Pork is sometimes chopped, spiced, and stuffed into stretchy tubes to make *sausages.* Another important pork product is *lard*—pork fat that has been melted and strained. It is used in cooking.

Uncooked pork may cause a disease called *trichinosis.* Pork should be thoroughly cooked before it is eaten.

Young hogs are called *pigs.* Pigs and hogs are raised in most countries of the world. Some religions, such as Judaism and Islam, forbid the eating of pork because they consider hogs unclean.

porpoise, *see* dolphins and porpoises

portrait

A portrait is a formal picture of a person. It can be a drawing, painting, sculpture, or photograph. A portrait shows what a person looked like and wore. It also shows something about the character of the person. We know what some famous people of the past looked like because we have portraits of them. For example, we know how George Washington looked from the portraits of him painted by Gilbert Stuart.

Some artists make portraits of themselves. These are called *self-portraits.* The artists Rembrandt and Van Gogh both painted self-portraits throughout their lives. These series of self-portraits show us how the artists changed as they aged. (*See* **Rembrandt van Rijn** and **Van Gogh, Vincent.**)

In the past, most portraits were of kings and queens and other important people. Today, nearly anyone can have his or her portrait captured in a photograph. In fact, one of the early uses of photography during the 1800s was for making portraits. The photographs taken by Mathew Brady of President Abraham Lincoln are among the most famous and beautiful photographic portraits.

See also **painters and painting; photography;** and **sculpture.**

Portugal

Capital: Lisbon	
Area: 35,553 square miles (92,082 square kilometers)	
Population (1985): about 10,046,000	
Official language: Portuguese	

Portugal is a small, beautiful country on the Iberian Peninsula in southwestern Europe. Spain occupies most of the peninsula. Portugal is on the peninsula's western side, facing the Atlantic Ocean.

Portuguese sailors and explorers, such as Bartolomeu Dias and Vasco da Gama, made daring voyages in the 1400s and 1500s. Soon, Portugal was a powerful trading nation, with colonies in South America, Africa, and Asia. Portuguese ships brought valuable spices, silks, and minerals back to Europe. One Portuguese colony, Brazil, became the largest country in South America. Brazil's official language is still Portuguese.

Portugal no longer has colonies. The Azores and Madeiras, two island groups in the Atlantic, are Portuguese territories. So is Macao, a small peninsula of China.

Sharp-prowed fishing boats at Nazare, a Portuguese village on the Atlantic shore.

ELEVATION

Feet
5000- 10000
2000- 5000
1000- 2000
0- 1000

0   50   100
Miles

Most Portuguese are either fishermen or farmers. Wine grapes are the main crop, and citrus fruits, olives, almonds, corn, and grains are among Portugal's other farm products. About one person in three lives in a city. Most people live in small villages.

Portugal's main industries are steel mills, shipbuilding, and petroleum. Food processing, cork production, and tourism are also important to Portugal's economy.

postal service

A nation's postal service handles and delivers mail. In the United States, this job is done by the United States Postal Service, a government agency. Post offices across the United States handle over 140 billion letters, magazines, packages, and other pieces of mail each year.

Post offices also sell stamps. To mail a letter, you place a stamp on it and drop it into a mailbox. A postal worker will collect all the letters from the mailbox and bring them to the nearest post office. There, they are sorted according to their addresses. Letters and packages going out of town are put into bags and sent to a large postal center. There, the stamps are *canceled*—marked with wavy lines so they cannot be used again. Next, each letter receives a *postmark*. The postmark states the name of the post office and the date and time the letter was handled.

The postmarked letters are again sorted by address. Mail going hundreds of miles is sent by airplane. Mail going shorter distances goes by train or truck. Letters are usually sent first class, which means they are delivered faster than most other mail.

These machines postmark first class mail and cancel the stamps.

potassium

The element potassium is a whitish metal. It was discovered and named by Sir Humphry Davy in 1807. He ran an electric current through *potash*—a substance made by boiling wood ashes. The electric current separated the potassium from the carbon and oxygen in the potash.

Potassium is very light, and so soft that it can be cut with a knife. When exposed to air or water, potassium reacts violently. It combines quickly with the elements in air and water, creating so much heat that a fire can start. Potassium compounds do not react this way with air and water.

All plants and animals need potassium. They get it from compounds. Plants, which need potassium to grow, get potassium compounds from the soil. Fruits and vegetables are a good source of potassium for animals, including people. Small quantities of potassium help us control our muscles.

Every year, the world uses about 25.7 billion kilograms (57 billion pounds) of potassium compounds. Most of it is potassium nitrate, which is used as a crop fertilizer. Other important potassium compounds are used to make glass, explosives, dyes, bleaches, medicines, and chemicals.

potato

The potato is one of the world's most important and popular vegetables. People eat potatoes baked, boiled, mashed, fried, or cooked with other foods. Many potatoes grown in the United States are made into potato chips and french fries.

Potato plants have leafy stems and purple, pink, or white flowers. The potatoes are *tubers* formed on the parts of the stems that grow underground. Most potatoes are white inside. Their skins are shades of brown or red. Sweet potatoes and yams, which are yellow or orange inside, are not potatoes. They come from thick root parts of two different kinds of plants.

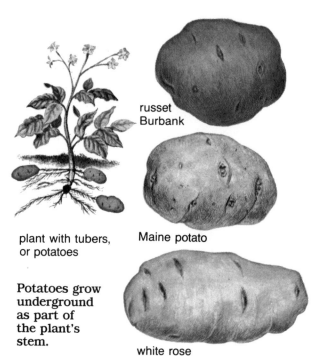

russet Burbank

plant with tubers, or potatoes

Maine potato

Potatoes grow underground as part of the plant's stem.

white rose

Almost four-fifths of a potato is water. The solid part is mostly starch. Potatoes are rich in vitamins B and C. They contain iron and potassium, among other minerals. Potatoes are also a good source of *protein,* a material the body uses for energy. Potatoes have very little fat. They can become fattening if they are fried, or served with butter or sour cream.

Most potatoes are planted from *seed potatoes.* These are tubers or tuber parts with at least one bud, called an *eye.* A stem grows from the eye, and a new plant grows from the stem. A fruit that looks like a tiny tomato grows on the flowering part of the potato plant. Some potatoes are grown from the fruits' seeds. Scientists also use the seeds to develop new kinds of potatoes.

The potato probably was first grown in the Andes Mountains of South America. Hundreds of years ago, the Inca living there dried potatoes and ground them into a flour called *chuño.* They used the chuño to bake bread. Today, the potato is still a very important food crop for the people who live in the Andes.

Potatoes were brought to Europe in the 1500s by Spanish explorers returning from South America. British explorers brought potatoes back to their country. European settlers brought potatoes to North America beginning in the 1600s. The potato grew so well in Ireland that it became known as the *Irish potato*.

For many years, potatoes were Ireland's most important crop. When a disease attacked the potato crop in Ireland in the early 1840s, hundreds of thousands of people starved to death. Thousands more came to the United States to start a new life.

pottery, *see* china and pottery

poultry

Birds raised for their meat or for their eggs are called poultry. In many countries, chickens are the most popular kind of poultry. Turkeys, ducks, and geese are other common kinds of poultry.

Chickens Most chickens in the United States are sold as *roasters, broilers,* or *fryers.* Broilers and fryers are young chickens from 9 to 12 weeks old. Roasters are chickens between 4 and 6 months old. Roasters are usually cooked whole. Broilers and fryers are often cut up and cooked.

Chicken parts—such as legs, wings, and breasts—are used in stews and other dishes. People use chopped chicken meat in soups and chicken salad. Food stores sell frankfurters made from chicken.

Many families living on small farms raise a few chickens for meat and eggs. Most broilers, fryers, and roasters sold in the United States come from very large chicken farms. Often, these farms also raise *laying hens*—female chickens raised just to produce eggs.

Some of the larger farms produce more than a million chickens a year. These farms are *automated.* This means that machines bring food and water to the chickens, which are kept in cages. To keep the chickens healthy, the cages are cleaned often and the birds are vaccinated. Their feed contains medicines. (*See* **vaccine.**)

Other Poultry Turkeys are usually raised outdoors in small, fenced-in areas. Most turkeys are too large for a family to eat at one meal. For this reason, turkeys were once served mostly on holidays, such as Thanksgiving, when large groups of people got together.

Today, turkey meat is popular all year round because of its pleasing flavor and low fat content. Turkey is often sold already cooked and sliced for sandwiches. Many food stores also sell fresh or frozen turkey parts, frozen dinners that include turkey, and canned soups that contain turkey.

Duck farms are usually smaller than chicken farms, but they are run in much the same way as chicken farms. Many ducks and geese are sold frozen. Cornish hens, guinea fowl, and pheasants are also kinds of poultry. They are raised on smaller farms.

Other Poultry Products Feathers from ducks and geese are used to stuff pillows, quilts, sleeping bags, and jackets. Eggs are used to make paint, varnishes, shampoos, and soaps. (*See* **egg.**)

Ducks, geese, pheasants, turkeys, and chickens are all poultry.

white peking duck

toulouse goose

chinese ring-necked pheasant

barred rock chicken

giant white turkey

The mother prairie dog at left has been marked with a harmless dye so that zoologists can follow her activities. The other prairie dogs are probably her young.

prairie

A prairie is an almost flat, treeless plain covered with grass. Prairies are found where there is not enough rain and snow for forests to grow, but where it is warm enough for grass to grow. Wildflowers, such as prairie lilies, prairie roses, and black-eyed Susans, also grow on prairies.

In North America, prairies stretch north to south down the middle of Canada and the United States. In South America, prairies called *pampas* cover a large part of Argentina and Uruguay. In Europe and Asia, the prairies with short grass are called *steppes*. They cover large areas of the Soviet Union. The African plain, called the *veld*, is another kind of prairie.

In the drier parts of the North American prairie, the common grasses are little bluestem, buffalo grass, side oats grama, and prairie dropseed. These grasses usually grow no taller than 1 meter (37 inches). The area where they grow is called the *short-grass prairie*. Switch grass, big bluestem, orchard grass, cordgrass, and gama grass grow in wetter prairies. These plants grow as tall as 3 meters (10 feet). The area where they grow is called the *tall-grass prairie*.

See also **plain** and **grassland.**

prairie dog

The prairie dog is a mammal that gets its name because it barks like a dog. It is not a dog, but a kind of squirrel. It is about 30 centimeters (1 foot) long. It has brownish fur that is darker on the back than on the belly.

Prairie dogs live on the plains of North America. They live in colonies, often called *prairie-dog towns.* A colony may contain thousands of prairie dogs.

These animals use their strong claws to dig underground burrows. They sleep in their burrows at night and are active during the day. When they are aboveground, a few keep watch while the others feed on grass, roots, and seeds. The guards sit up on their hind legs and watch for hawks, coyotes, and other enemies. If one of the guards sees an enemy, it warns the others by barking. Then all the prairie dogs jump into their deep burrows. They stay hidden until the danger passes.

Prairie-dog burrows have special rooms. One room is for storing food. Another room is lined with soft grass. Female prairie dogs give birth to their babies there. The newborn babies are very tiny and cannot see or hear. But they grow quickly, and are full-size by the time they are six months old.

prescription

Many powerful medicines cannot be bought without a prescription—a doctor's written permission. A prescription states the name of the patient, the name of the medicine, and the amount the patient may buy. It also tells how often to take the medicine and how much to take each time. Prescriptions are also written for eyeglasses, special shoes, and medical equipment and treatments.

When writing a prescription, a doctor considers the patient's age, weight, and past health problems, as well as the illness. It is important that the prescription be used only by the person for whom it was written. The same medicine that may be helpful for one person, may be harmful to another.

The patient takes the prescription to a *pharmacy*—a drugstore. There, a *pharmacist*—a person especially trained to prepare medicines—fills the prescription. He or she measures out the medicine and labels it with the patient's name, the doctor's name, the date, and directions for taking it. The patient should follow these directions carefully. Prescription medicines can be dangerous if they are not properly used. If the patient has any questions, he or she should always ask the doctor or pharmacist to answer them.

The federal government controls the making and selling of prescription medicines. People who illegally make or sell these medicines can be severely punished.

See also **drugs and medicines.**

At left, a prescription written by a doctor. At right, a pharmacist *fills* the prescription just as the doctor ordered.

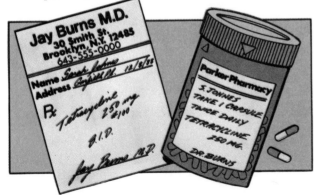

preservative

A preservative is a substance that helps keep food from spoiling. *Microorganisms*—tiny living things such as molds, bacteria, and yeasts—cause food to spoil. Preservatives keep these microorganisms from growing. Food treated with preservatives can be safely stored longer than untreated food.

Salt and sugar are important food preservatives. Meat and fish are often treated with salt. Jams, jellies, and fruits are preserved by cooking them with sugar. Vitamins C and E are also sometimes used to preserve food.

Many foods are treated with other chemicals. Packaged meats may contain nitrites and nitrates to keep them from spoiling.

Salt or sugar preserve many foods. Other preservatives are listed on food labels.

Some stores spray sulfites on fruits and vegetables to keep them fresh-looking. BHA and BHT keep breakfast cereals and other boxed foods fresh.

Some chemical preservatives may not be good for people. For example, some people are allergic to sulfites. Other chemicals may cause illness after years of eating them. Scientists are testing these substances to be sure they are safe.

Refrigeration, freezing, and canning can preserve foods without adding chemicals. So can a newer method called *irradiation.* Foods are exposed to high-energy X rays to kill the bacteria in them. Irradiation is being tested to be sure it does not damage foods or make them unsafe.

See also **food processing.**

presidents of the United States

Presidents have headed the United States in an unbroken line since George Washington became the first president on April 30, 1789. The office of president was created in 1788, when the Constitution of the United States was adopted. The Constitution created three branches of the federal government—the legislative, the executive, and the judicial. The president is the *chief executive*—head of the executive branch of government. The president is also the *head of state*—the leader of the entire nation.

A person who runs for president must be a U.S. citizen born in the United States and at least 35 years old. A presidential term lasts four years. No president may be elected to more than two terms. A president is elected with a vice president. If the president dies or resigns, the vice president becomes president until the end of that term.

Every four years, on the Tuesday after the first Monday in November, people who are registered voters go to the polls to vote for president. Any number of people may run for president. Usually, there are two major candidates, one from each major political party—Democratic and Republican. In the months before the election, the candidates travel all over the country. They make speeches and appear on television and radio. They tell people their ideas and try to persuade voters to choose them as president. When the election comes, the voters decide which candidate becomes president.

But the voters do not decide the winner directly. Their votes elect representatives called *electors* to a group named the electoral college. Even though the candidates' names appear on the ballot, the voters are really choosing electors. Each state has as many votes in the electoral college as the state sends to Congress. The District of Columbia has three votes. It is actually the electoral college that chooses the president.

The president of the United States has a number of powers and responsibilities. The

President Reagan takes the oath of office in 1984 for his second term.

president proposes laws to Congress and keeps Congress informed about the condition of the country.

All bills passed by Congress must go to the president for approval. Bills that are approved become law. But a president may *veto* a bill. Then the bill goes back to Congress. There it must win the approval of two-thirds of Congress to *override* the president's veto and become law.

The president is commander in chief of the nation's military forces. He or she names the heads of executive government departments, appoints ministers to foreign countries, and nominates federal judges. The president also conducts the nation's relations with foreign countries and makes treaties and agreements with them.

The Presidential Inauguration Presidents are elected in November of election years. They do not take office until they are *inaugurated*—sworn in—the following year. Inauguration Day was March 4 for the first 32 presidents. But with the inauguration of the 33rd president, Harry S. Truman, the date of Inauguration Day was changed to January 20.

On Inauguration Day, the person who was elected president in November takes the oath of office and becomes the new president. The ceremony takes place outside the Capitol

Building in Washington, D.C. The president-elect places his or her right hand on the Bible, faces the chief justice of the Supreme Court, and repeats the oath as stated in the Constitution:

I do solemnly swear (or affirm) that I will faithfully execute the Office of President of the United States, and will to the best of my ability, preserve, protect, and defend the Constitution of the United States.

George Washington was the first president to take this oath. When he finished, he added, "So help me God." Since then, other presidents have added these words to the oath, too.

The Presidential Cabinet A number of departments have been established to help the president. The heads of these departments make up the presidential cabinet and are part of the executive branch of the government. They are not elected by the people. They are chosen by the president as advisers. During Washington's presidency, there were five departments. Today, there are 13. The head of each department is usually called its *secretary.* The justice department is headed by the attorney general.

The presidents of the United States are listed in the table. Those presidents with an asterisk (*) by their name have an entry in this encyclopedia.

See also **Constitution of the United States; Congress, United States; Supreme Court, United States;** and **United States history.**

PRESIDENTS OF THE UNITED STATES

Name, dates in office, party, vice president(s)	Personal	Highlights of Career
1. **George Washington*** April 30, 1789-March 4, 1797 Party: (none) Vice President: John Adams	Born February 1732, Virginia. Died there December 1799. Educated at home and trained as surveyor and soldier.	Commander of American Army in Revolutionary War. Chairman of Constitutional Convention. As president, united the new nation.
2. **John Adams*** March 4, 1797-March 4, 1801 Party: Federalist Vice President: Thomas Jefferson	Born October 1735, Massachusetts. Died there July 1826. Studied at Harvard University. Lawyer.	First vice president. As president, prevented war with France. First president to live in White House.
3. **Thomas Jefferson*** March 4, 1801-March 4, 1809 Party: Democratic-Republican Vice Presidents: Aaron Burr, George Clinton	Born April 1743, Virginia. Died there July 1826. Educated at College of William and Mary. Lawyer.	Wrote Declaration of Independence. First secretary of State. As president, doubled nation's size with Louisiana Purchase.
4. **James Madison** March 4, 1809-March 4, 1817 Party: Democratic-Republican Vice Presidents: George Clinton, Elbridge Gerry	Born March 1751, Virginia. Died there June 1836. Graduated from College of New Jersey (now Princeton University). Lawyer.	Influenced the writing of the U.S. Constitution. President during the War of 1812. Had to flee White House when British attacked.
5. **James Monroe** March 4, 1817-March 4, 1825 Party: Democratic-Republican Vice President: Daniel D. Tompkins	Born April 1758, Virginia. Died July 1831, New York. Studied law at College of William and Mary.	Congressman and senator. Secretary of State. As president, warned Europe in Monroe Doctrine to stay out of North and South American affairs.
6. **John Quincy Adams*** March 4, 1825-March 4, 1829 Party: Democratic-Republican Vice President: John C. Calhoun	Born July 1767, Massachusetts. Died February 1848, Washington, D.C. Graduated from Harvard University. Lawyer.	Senator. Secretary of State. As president, wanted Congress to pay for roads, canals, a national university, and a weather service. Later served 17 years in Congress.

Presidents with an * after their names have entries in the *Golden Book Encyclopedia.*

Name, dates in office, party, vice president(s)	Personal	Highlights of Career
7. **Andrew Jackson*** March 4, 1829-March 4, 1837 Party: Democrat Vice Presidents: John C. Calhoun, Martin Van Buren	Born March 1767, South Carolina. Died June 1845, Tennessee. Lawyer. War of 1812 hero. Defeated Creek and Seminole Indians.	Congressman and senator. As president, established "spoils system," rewarding supporters by giving them government jobs. Opposed national bank.
8. **Martin Van Buren** March 4, 1837-March 4, 1841 Party: Democrat Vice President: Richard M. Johnson	Born December 1782, New York. Died July 1862, New York. Lawyer.	State public official. Senator. Governor of New York. Secretary of State. Vice president. President during a period of economic hard times.
9. **William H. Harrison** March 4, 1841-April 4, 1841 Party: Whig Vice President: John Tyler	Born February 1773, Virginia. Died April 1841, Washington, D.C. Graduated from Hampden-Sydney College. Served in War of 1812.	Governor of Indiana Territory. Congressman and senator. First president to campaign for office. Died of pneumonia just one month after inauguration.
10. **John Tyler** April 6, 1841-March 4, 1845 Party: Whig Vice President: (none)	Born March 1790, Virginia. Died there January 1862. Graduated from College of William and Mary. Lawyer.	Congressman. Governor of Virginia. Senator. Vice president. Became president when Harrison died. Signed bill that led to Texas joining the United States.
11. **James K. Polk** March 4, 1845-March 4, 1849 Party: Democrat Vice President: George M. Dallas	Born November 1795, North Carolina. Died June 1849, Tennessee. Graduated from University of North Carolina. Lawyer.	Speaker of House of Representatives. Governor of Tennessee. As president, sent in troops to begin Mexican War and gain California and the Southwest.
12. **Zachary Taylor** March 5, 1849-July 9, 1850 Party: Whig Vice President: Millard Fillmore	Born November 1784, Virginia. Died July 1850, Washington, D.C. Received little formal schooling. Mexican War hero. Nicknamed "Old Rough and Ready."	As president, supported admission of California to United States as a nonslave state. Died in office.
13. **Millard Fillmore** July 10, 1850-March 4, 1853 Party: Whig Vice President: (none)	Born January 1800, New York. Died March 1874, New York. Taught in country schools. Lawyer.	New York State legislator. Congressman. Vice president. Favored Compromise of 1850 to settle dispute over slavery in newly settled territory.
14. **Franklin Pierce** March 4, 1853-March 4, 1857 Party: Democrat Vice President: William R. King	Born November 1804, New Hampshire. Died there October 1869. Graduated from Bowdoin College. Lawyer. Served in Mexican War.	Congressman and senator. As president, signed Kansas-Nebraska Act, which placed slavery under local rather than national law. Extended the U.S. southern border.
15. **James Buchanan** March 4, 1857-March 4, 1861 Party: Democrat Vice President: John Breckinridge	Born April 1791, Pennsylvania. Died there June 1868. Graduated from Dickinson College. Lawyer. Served in War of 1812.	Congressman. Minister to Russia, Britain. Senator. Secretary of State. Wanted *popular sovereignty* — the vote of the people — to settle slavery question in new states. Opposed secession.
16. **Abraham Lincoln*** March 4, 1861-April 15, 1865 Party: Republican Vice Presidents: Hannibal Hamlin, Andrew Johnson	Born February 1809, Kentucky. Died April 1865, Washington, D.C. Lawyer.	Illinois State legislator. Congressman. President during Civil War. Signed Emancipation Proclamation to free slaves. Assassinated.

Name, dates in office, party, vice president(s)	Personal	Highlights of Career
17. Andrew Johnson April 15, 1865-March 4, 1869 Party: National Union Vice President: (none)	Born December 1808, North Carolina. Died July 1875, Tennessee. Apprenticed as a tailor and taught himself to read.	Congressman. Governor of Tennessee. Senator. Vice president. Only president ever impeached — charged with crimes — but not convicted of conspiring against Congress.
18. Ulysses S. Grant* March 4, 1869-March 4, 1877 Party: Republican Vice Presidents: Schuyler Colfax, Henry Wilson	Born April 1822, Ohio. Died July 1885, New York. Graduated from U.S. Military Academy at West Point. Served in Mexican War.	Commander of Union forces in Civil War. As president, supported 15th Amendment, which promised black men the right to vote.
19. Rutherford B. Hayes March 4, 1877-March 4, 1881 Party: Republican Vice President: William A. Wheeler	Born October 1822, Ohio. Died there January 1893. Graduated from Kenyon College and Harvard Law School. Lawyer. Served in Civil War.	Congressman. Governor of Ohio. Won presidency in disputed election. As president, ended Northern troop occupation of Southern states, ending Reconstruction.
20. James A. Garfield March 4, 1881-September 19, 1881 Party: Republican Vice President: Chester A. Arthur	Born November 1831, Ohio. Died September 1881, New Jersey. Graduated from Williams College. Teacher. Served in Civil War.	Congressman. As president, fought against "spoils system." Assassinated after only six months in office.
21. Chester A. Arthur September 20, 1881-March 4, 1885 Party: Republican Vice President: (none)	Born October 1829, Vermont. Died November 1886, New York. Graduated from Union College. Teacher and lawyer. Served in Civil War.	Vice president. As president, signed into law the Civil Service Reform Act of 1883. Began rebuilding U.S. Navy.
22. Grover C. Cleveland March 4, 1885-March 4, 1889 Party: Democrat Vice President: Thomas A. Hendricks	Born March 1837, New Jersey. Died there June 1908. Lawyer.	Mayor of Buffalo, New York. Governor of New York. As president, dealt with unrest among nation's farmers and laborers, reformed currency system.
23. Benjamin Harrison March 4, 1889-March 4, 1893 Party: Republican Vice President: Levi P. Morton	Born August 1833, Ohio. Died March 1901, Indiana. Graduated from Miami University of Ohio. Lawyer. Served in Civil War.	Senator. As president, supported passage of Sherman Antitrust Act to reduce power of large businesses. Expanded pension benefits for Civil War veterans.

William Henry Harrison (the 9th president) was the grandfather of Benjamin Harrison, who became the 23rd president.

Grover Cleveland was president twice, in 1885-89 and in 1893-97.

Name, dates in office, party, vice president(s)	Personal	Highlights of Career
24. **Grover C. Cleveland** March 4, 1893-March 4, 1897 Party: Democrat Vice President: Adlai E. Stevenson	Born March 1837, New Jersey. Died there June 1908. Lawyer.	Mayor of Buffalo, New York. Governor of New York. As president, sent U.S. troops to Illinois to end strike against Pullman Company.
25. **William McKinley** March 4, 1897-September 14, 1901 Party: Republican Vice Presidents: Garret A. Hobart, Theodore Roosevelt	Born January 1843, Ohio. Died September 1901, New York. Lawyer. Served in Civil War.	Congressman. Governor of Ohio. As president, called for declaration of war against Spain after sinking of U.S. battleship *Maine*. Assassinated.
26. **Theodore Roosevelt*** September 14, 1901-March 4, 1909 Party: Republican Vice President: Charles W. Fairbanks	Born October 1858, New York. Died there January 1919. Graduated from Harvard University. Rancher. Writer. Spanish-American War hero.	Assistant secretary of Navy. Governor of New York. Vice president. As president, began building of Panama Canal. Won Nobel Peace Prize.
27. **William H. Taft** March 4, 1909-March 4, 1913 Party: Republican Vice President: James S. Sherman	Born September 1857, Ohio. Died March 1930, Washington, D.C. Graduated from Yale University and Cincinnati Law School. Lawyer.	Secretary of War. Governor of Philippines. Broke up big business monopolies. Supported creation of federal income tax. Chief justice of U.S. Supreme Court.
28. **Woodrow Wilson** March 4, 1913-March 4, 1921 Party: Democrat Vice President: Thomas R. Marshall	Born December 1856, Virginia. Died February 1924, Washington, D.C. Graduated from Princeton and Johns Hopkins universities. Professor and president of Princeton.	Governor of New Jersey. President during World War I. Worked on peace treaty based on Fourteen Points for world peace. Won Nobel Peace Prize.
29. **Warren G. Harding** March 4, 1921-August 2, 1923 Party: Republican Vice President: Calvin Coolidge	Born November 1865, Ohio. Died August 1923, California. Owner and publisher of a newspaper — the Marion, Ohio, *Star*.	Senator. As president, held Washington Conference, which placed limits on worldwide arms. Died in office.
30. **Calvin Coolidge** August 2, 1923-March 4, 1929 Party: Republican Vice President: Charles G. Dawes	Born July 1872, Vermont. Died January 1933, Massachusetts. Graduated from Amherst College. Lawyer.	Governor of Massachusetts. Vice president. As president, believed that "the business of American is business" and approved laws that encouraged business growth.
31. **Herbert Hoover** March 4, 1929-March 4, 1933 Party: Republican Vice President: Charles Curtis	Born August 1874, Iowa. Died October 1964, New York. Graduated from Stanford University. Mining Engineer.	President during Great Depression. Opposed federal programs for unemployed, but approved extending loans to banks and big businesses.
32. **Franklin D. Roosevelt*** March 4, 1933-April 12, 1945 Party: Democrat Vice Presidents: John N. Garner, Henry A. Wallace, Harry S. Truman	Born January 1882, New York. Died April 1945, Georgia. Graduated from Harvard University and attended Columbia Law School. Lawyer.	Assistant secretary of Navy. Governor of New York. As president, began New Deal to ease Great Depression. President during World War II. Died in office.
33. **Harry S. Truman*** April 12, 1945-January 20, 1953 Party: Democrat Vice President: Alben W. Barkley	Born May 1884, Missouri. Died there December 1972. Served in World War I. Studied law at Kansas City Law School.	Senator. Vice president. Ordered dropping of atomic bomb to end World War II. Created NATO. Approved Marshall Plan to help war-torn Europe recover.

Name, dates in office, party, vice president(s)	Personal	Highlights of Career
34. **Dwight D. Eisenhower*** January 20, 1953-January 20, 1961 Party: Republican Vice President: Richard M. Nixon	Born October 1890, Texas. Died March 1969, Washington, D.C. Graduated from U.S. Military Academy at West Point. Rose to five-star general in World War II.	Supreme Allied commander in World War II. President of Columbia University. As president, ended Korean War, enforced laws to end racial separation in schools.
35. **John Fitzgerald Kennedy*** January 20, 1961-November 22, 1963 Party: Democrat Vice President: Lyndon B. Johnson	Born May 1917, Massachusetts. Died November 1963, Texas. Graduated from Harvard University. Wounded in World War II.	Congressman. Senator. As president, surrounded Cuba to make Soviet Union remove missiles there. Began the U.S. space program. Assassinated.
36. **Lyndon B. Johnson*** November 22, 1963-January 20, 1969 Party: Democrat Vice President: Hubert H. Humphrey	Born August 1908, in Texas. Died there January 1973. Graduated from Southwest Texas State Teachers College. Served in World War II.	Congressman. Senator. Vice president. As president, started Great Society program to erase poverty. Expanded U.S. involvement in Vietnam War.
37. **Richard M. Nixon*** January 20, 1969-August 9, 1974 Party: Republican Vice Presidents: Spiro T. Agnew, Gerald R. Ford	Born January 1913, California. Graduated from Whittier College and Duke University Law School. Lawyer. Served in World War II.	Congressman. Senator. Vice president. As president, ended Vietnam War and renewed relations with China. Resigned from office over Watergate scandal.
38. **Gerald R. Ford*** August 9, 1974-January 20, 1977 Party: Republican Vice President: Nelson A. Rockefeller	Born July 1913, Nebraska. Graduated from University of Michigan and Yale University Law School. Lawyer. Served in World War II.	Congressman. Vice president. As president, pardoned President Nixon for his part in Watergate scandal. Only president not elected either president or vice president.
39. **Jimmy Carter*** January 20, 1977-January 20, 1981 Party: Democrat Vice President: Walter F. Mondale	Born October 1924, Georgia. Graduated from U.S. Naval Academy at Annapolis. Served as officer aboard nuclear submarines. Peanut farmer.	Governor of Georgia. As president, worked out peace treaty between Israel and Egypt, supported protection of human rights throughout the world.
40. **Ronald W. Reagan*** January 20, 1981- Party: Republican Vice President: George H. W. Bush	Born February 1911, Illinois. Graduated from Eureka College. Radio sports announcer and movie actor. Served in World War II.	Governor of California. As president, cut taxes and encouraged business growth and defense spending. Signed nuclear disarmament treaty with Soviet Union.

William Howard Taft was the biggest president—he weighed about 300 pounds.

Franklin Roosevelt served longest of any president— just over 12 years.

John F. Kennedy was the youngest man ever elected president—43 years old.

Scientist Joseph Priestley discovered the element oxygen in the late 1700s.

Priestley, Joseph

Joseph Priestley was an English scientist and church minister. He is known as the discoverer of oxygen.

Priestley was born in 1733. As a young man, he studied languages and religion and became a minister. In 1766, he met Benjamin Franklin and they became friends. Priestley, like Franklin, turned his attention to science.

Priestley first studied electricity. Then he became interested in gases. He started doing experiments and discovered carbon dioxide. When he dissolved some of this gas in water, he came up with a funny new drink—called *soda water* or *seltzer*. Next he discovered nitrous oxide—"laughing gas." Some dentists use this gas to stop pain. (*See* **anesthetic.**)

Priestley was actually not the first to discover oxygen. A Swedish scientist, Karl Scheele, had already found it, but his work was not known. Priestley made oxygen by heating mercuric oxide—a compound of mercury and oxygen. The heated mercuric oxide broke down into mercury and oxygen. (*See* **oxygen.**)

Priestley's political and religious ideas made him unpopular in England. In 1794, he moved to the United States. He died in Pennsylvania in 1804.

Prince Edward Island

Capital: Charlottetown
Area: 2,180 square miles (5,646 square kilometers) (smallest province)
Population (1981): 122,506 (1985): about 126,800 (smallest province)
Became a province: July 1, 1873 (7th province)

Prince Edward Island is Canada's smallest province and the only one completely separated from the mainland. Thousands of tourists visit the island's sunny beaches and old fishing villages each year.

Prince Edward Island lies in the Gulf of St. Lawrence—an arm of the Atlantic Ocean—just off Canada's eastern coast. It is one of the Atlantic Provinces—along with New Brunswick, Nova Scotia, and Newfoundland. The province is bordered on the south and east by Nova Scotia, and it faces New

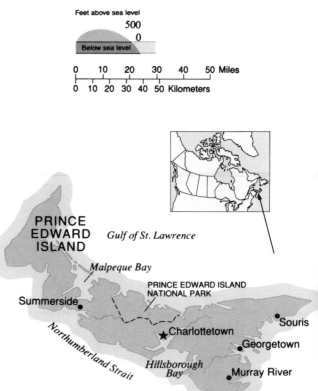

Brunswick on the west. The Micmac Indians, the first people to live on the island, named it *Abegweit*—meaning "sheltered in the sea" or "home cradled on the waves."

Land The coast of Prince Edward Island has many bays. The Hillsborough and Malpeque bays cut nearly all the way through the island. The northern coast has cocoa-colored, sandy beaches that rise to low dunes. The southern coast is more rugged, with low cliffs of red sandstone.

Rolling hills cover much of the land. There are some forests, but most of the island is farmland or pastureland. The soil is deep red, fertile, and easy to plow because there are few rocks. For this reason, Prince Edward Island is known as the "Garden of the Gulf." Potatoes are the main crop. Beef and dairy products are also important.

The island's fishermen catch lobster, cod, herring, mackerel, and clams. The oysters found in Malpeque Bay in the northern part of the province are among the best-tasting in the world. Prince Edward Island is one of the leading oyster producers of North America.

History Jacques Cartier landed on the island in 1534 and claimed it for France. In 1603, Samuel de Champlain named the island Ile St. Jean. The French began to settle there in the 1700s.

France gave Ile St. Jean to the British in 1763, after the French and Indian War had ended. The island was at first a part of Nova Scotia. It became a separate colony in 1769. In 1799, the island was renamed in honor of Prince Edward Augustus, the son of Britain's King George III. The capital city was named Charlottetown after Prince Edward's mother, Queen Charlotte Sophia.

People Although Prince Edward Island has a small population, it has more people per square mile than any other province. Almost three-quarters of the island's people live on farms or in small villages. Four-fifths of the people are of British descent, and most of the rest are of French origin. There are also several hundred Micmac Indians on the island.

The province's capital and only city, Charlottetown, is located on Hillsborough Bay on the southern coast. Half of all of the manufacturing on Prince Edward Island takes place in Charlottetown. Blankets are woven from the wool of island sheep. Fish and farm products are processed and canned in the city's factories. Charlottetown's harbor is open almost all year.

Charlottetown is called the "Cradle of Confederation," because representatives from several British colonies in North America met there in 1864 to make plans to unite. As a result of this meeting, the Dominion of Canada was created in 1867. Prince Edward Island joined the new nation in 1873.

A lighthouse and some lobster traps in a seaside village on Prince Edward Island.

printing

Printed words and pictures seem to be everywhere—in books, newspapers, and magazines, on packages, bags, soda cans, and posters. But just 500 years ago, printed words and pictures were rare.

One of the first printed books was made in China around the year 900. It was made by *block printing.* A mirror image of a page was

To see how a letterpress works, carve a picture on a potato slice, put ink on the raised surface, then press onto paper.

cut into a block of wood. Ink was spread over the block, and then it was pressed onto paper to make a printed page. The block could be used to print several copies of the same page. But carving a new block for each page took a long time.

Movable Type Around the year 1440, printing by *movable type* was first used in Europe. Johannes Gutenberg usually gets credit for this invention, although movable type had already been used by the Chinese. Gutenberg made type for individual letters by pouring metal into molds. He made several pieces for every letter of the alphabet. Each piece of type is a raised mirror image of what the letter will look like when printed. To make up the words and sentences to be printed, the letters were set in reverse order. The lines of type for each page were held in place by a wooden frame. The raised print was coated with ink, and paper was pressed over it. On the paper, the printed words were in the correct order and could be easily read. (*See* **Gutenberg, Johannes.**)

Instead of having to cut a new wood block for each page, printers could quickly set pages with individual letter type. Many copies of a set page could be printed. Then the type could be re-used to make up other pages.

Printing Presses Printing is done on a *press.* The first presses were *platen presses.* They had a flat surface, called a *bed,* and a heavy plate, called a *platen,* which could be cranked up and down. A frame of set type

On a four-color printing press, the paper is printed on both sides four times (each time in a different color). It is then cut, folded, and gathered.

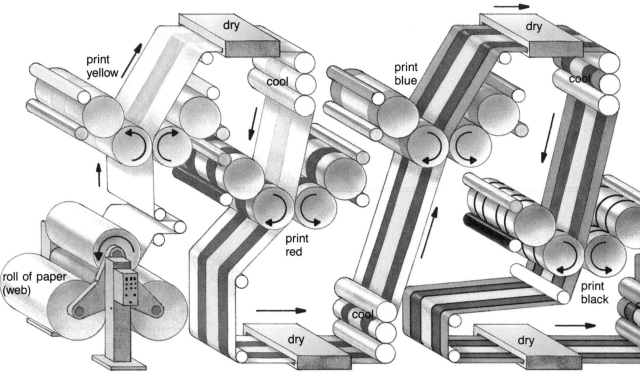

was placed on the bed and wiped with ink. Paper was laid over the raised, inked type. The platen was lowered onto the paper, pressing it against the type.

A steam-powered printing press was invented in 1811. It made printing faster and easier. But even with steam power, presses still worked in very much the same way.

A big improvement came in 1846 when Richard Hoe invented a *rotary press.* The rotary press has two cylinders instead of a bed and platen. One cylinder is set with the type to be printed, and the other is blank. Paper is fed between the rolling cylinders. The blank cylinder presses the paper against the inked typeset cylinder. The rotary press made printing faster—especially when printers later began using rolls of paper instead of sheets. Most newspapers and books are printed on rotary presses.

The *flatbed press* uses a flat bed and a cylinder. The type is on the flat bed, and the paper is rolled over the type by a large cylinder.

Flatbed presses are used to print boxes, cartons, and some kinds of books.

The platen press, the flatbed press, and the rotary press all use movable raised type. Printing done on these presses is called *letterpress,* because the raised letters are pressed against the paper.

Other Ways of Printing *Gravure* printing does not use raised or movable type. Letters are *engraved*—carved—in a metal plate. Ink is applied to the engraved plate. The surface is wiped so the ink remains only in the engraved places. A roller presses the paper against the plate and into the inky grooves.

Offset lithography is different from letterpress and gravure printing. The type is first set by letterpress or photographic methods, and then photographed. The photograph is developed onto a cylinder plate. The cylinder plate is coated with chemicals that stick only where there is an image. Ink is then applied to the plate, and it sticks only to the chemicals. The cylinder plate is rolled against a rubber cylinder. This transfers the inked image to the rubber cylinder. The rubber cylinder then rolls over the paper and prints the page. Offset lithography is used to print many books and magazines, and other things, such as cartons and labels. It can be used for black-and-white or color printing.

Most color printing is done by printing a layer of tiny dots on top of one or more other layers of tiny dots. Usually, there are four layers—red, yellow, blue, and black. The colors we see printed depend on how many dots there are in each layer, how close together they are, and where they are in relation to the dots in the other layers. (*See* **color.**)

Printing both sides of a paper is done one side at a time. With platen and flatbed presses, the paper must be removed and the ink must dry before the other side can be printed. Large rotary and lithographic presses have sets of printing cylinders, working in order, to print one side and then the other without interruption.

Mimeograph and *photocopy* machines are useful for printing a small number of

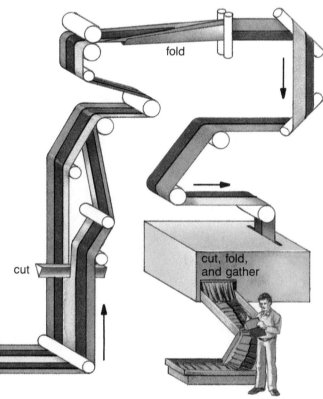

fold

cut

cut, fold, and gather

copies—usually no more than 100 copies at a time. A photocopy machine is often used to make a single copy. (*See* **photocopier.**)

Silkscreen is another printing method that is often used to produce posters and artwork. Ink or paint is applied through cut-out letters and designs.

Today, lasers and computers are being used to make printing better, faster and less expensive. (*See* **laser.**)

See also **books.**

prison

A prison is a place that houses adults who have been found guilty of serious crimes. Criminals who live in prisons are called *inmates* or *convicts.* They spend a certain amount of time in prison as punishment for such serious crimes as murder, kidnapping, and armed robbery. *Jails* are places where people are kept for shorter periods of time. Some of these people have been accused of crimes and are awaiting trial. Some have been convicted of crimes but will spend less than a year in jail.

The United States has about 3,500 city and county jails, 800 state prisons, and 40 federal prisons. The biggest federal prisons include those at Lexington, Kentucky; Atlanta, Georgia; and Leavenworth, Kansas. In the late 1980s, U.S. jails and prisons held about 460,000 inmates.

Prisons in the United States are divided into three types. *Maximum-security prisons* house the most dangerous criminals. These prisons are heavily guarded. They hold inmates who may try to escape, cause riots, or harm other prisoners. *Moderate-security prisons* are for inmates who are not as dangerous and need less control. Inmates sent to *minimum-security prisons* are considered more trustworthy and sometimes even work outside the prison.

The main prison buildings are called *cell blocks.* They contain many *cells*—small rooms with high ceilings and steel bars. Each cell holds one or two prisoners. A cell usually has one or more beds, a toilet, and a sink. The cell blocks often surround a yard where prisoners exercise. Prisons also have dining halls, a laundry, a chapel, a school, and a library. Some prisons have factories or farms where inmates work. The prison is surrounded by walls with towers where guards stand watch.

Prisons also offer *rehabilitation* programs to prepare prisoners for when they are out of prison. These include school courses and job training. Social workers and doctors try to help prisoners solve their problems.

Prisoners who disobey prison rules are sometimes sent to a small cell called the *hole.* While there, they are kept apart from other inmates and given little to eat. A prisoner who shows good behavior may be made a *trusty.* A trusty is allowed to work outside the prison and live in a special area. Good behavior may also earn a prisoner *parole*—an early release from prison.

See also **crime.**

A traditional prison block at the Joliet Correctional Center in Illinois.

probability

Probability is the part of mathematics that deals with the chance or possibility of something happening. No one can be certain what will happen in the future. But learning about probability helps people make good guesses.

When you flip a coin, have you ever wondered what the chances are that it will turn up heads? You can make a good guess if you use probability. Here is how.

First, count how many different ways the coin can land. There are two possible outcomes—the coin either lands heads up or it lands tails up. Second, count how many of those possible outcomes will be successful ones. There is only one successful outcome—heads up. Now, compare these two numbers by making a *ratio*. A ratio compares the number of successful outcomes to the total number of possible outcomes. In this case the ratio is 1 to 2. This ratio may be written as a fraction—1/2.

Suppose you have four red marbles and five blue marbles in a bag. What are the chances that when you pick a marble without looking, it will turn out to be a blue one?

First, count the total number of possible outcomes. There are nine possibilities, because there are nine marbles—four red and five blue. How many of these possibilities are what you want? The answer is five, because there are five blue marbles. Your ratio, then, of successful choices to total number of possible choices, is 5 to 9. Written as a fraction, it is 5/9.

Now, can you figure the probability for choosing a red marble? When you follow the steps we used above, your answer will be 4 to 9, or 4/9.

A good way to check your answers when you work with probability is to add the probability of the successful choice to the probability of the unsuccessful choice. The sum should be 1. If you add the probabilities for choosing a blue marble (5/9) and a red marble (4/9), you get 9/9, which is equal to 1.

Probability is an important part of mathematics. It helps scientists and other experts to make good guesses and to plan and build things based on these guesses.

A PROBABILITY TESTER

A ball falls from the top, hitting a series of knobs. Each time, it has an even chance of falling to the left or to the right. Finally, it falls into one of 14 slots. The ball is most likely to fall into one of the middle slots, because there are many possible routes it can follow to a middle slot. Only one possible route brings the ball to the slot on the far left or the far right.

These students are using a production line to produce a class newspaper. Some write, some make copies, some staple and fold.

production line

You and three friends must put together and staple 30 copies of a three-page notice for your class. You would probably start by arranging the pages into three stacks, one stack for each of the three pages. One friend would pass a copy of page 1 to the next friend. That person would put it on top of a copy of page 2 and pass both pages to the third person. This person would add page 3 behind page 2 and hand the set to you for stapling. Soon, you would have 30 stapled copies of the notice.

This way of working is a simple production line—also called an *assembly line.* Each person does one part of the job, over and over, to get the whole job done more quickly.

Breaking up a job into smaller jobs done by a number of workers is called *division of labor.* For thousands of years, people have worked this way to farm, hunt, and build. But a modern production line is different in two ways. It has *specialized machinery* and assembles *standardized parts.*

The pages you put together for the notice were standardized—they were all the same size. Specialized machinery at a paper factory makes it possible to cut millions of pages the same size. The stapler you used is a specialized machine, too.

Christopher Polhem, of Sweden, was one of the first people to use division of labor, standardized parts, and specialized machines together. In 1700, he built a factory that made all sorts of metal products—from nails, pins, and screws to finished locks and clocks. He hired skilled workers who were experienced at working specialized machines to do particular jobs on the assembly line. Polhem's factory turned out hundreds of finished products each day.

People continued to improve the production line. In the 1780s, a French gunmaker designed machines that could make standardized gun parts—gun parts that were exactly alike. A trigger that had been made one day could be assembled with a barrel made the day before and with other parts. The other parts could have been made months before, or the day after the trigger was made. Any barrel could fit with any hammer, firing pin, stock, or handle. A gun with a broken part could be fixed with a ready-made replacement part.

Standardized parts were also known as *interchangeable parts.* The American inventor Eli Whitney manufactured interchangeable parts for the cotton gin and also for guns. By 1807, his factory production lines were turning out thousands of guns each year. Each gun had as many as 50 parts. Any part

from one model of a gun fit any other gun of the same model. (*See* **Whitney, Eli.**)

Having interchangeable parts makes it far easier and less expensive to repair many products. This is because the broken part alone can be removed and fixed or replaced. You can buy new brake pads for your bicycle, or a new wheel for your skateboard. You do not have to save up to buy a whole new bicycle or skateboard.

Henry Ford set up one of the first automobile production lines in 1913. His workers could assemble a car, from start to finish, in just an hour and a half. Ford used division of labor, specialized machinery, and standardized parts on his production line.

The production line is part of *mass production*—the process of manufacturing products in great numbers. Ford found that the more cars he could produce, the cheaper each one could be. For example, in 1912, Ford's company sold fewer than 80,000 cars, and each one cost about $700. Five years later, in 1917, 750,000 cars were produced on the Ford production line. Each car sold for less than $400. Ford could also sell spare parts, which car owners could buy if a car needed to be repaired. (*See* **Ford, Henry.**)

A worker on an automobile production line controls the work of a robot. The robot does several jobs on each car body that passes by.

prophet

A prophet is a special kind of religious leader. The prophets spoke out when they thought people were not living the way God wanted them to live. The prophets challenged peoples and nations to change the way they behaved. Some prophets predicted what would happen in the future.

Most prophets were not very popular. They had to tell kings and other powerful leaders that they were wrong. Some prophets were punished or even killed. But prophets believed that they spoke for God, and so they had great courage.

Prophets are important in the Jewish, Christian, and Islamic faiths. Jews think of Moses as the first prophet. He brought the Ten Commandments to the Hebrews—the ancestors of the Jews, who lived in the land later called Israel. Centuries after Moses, the prophet Jeremiah warned an evil king to change his ways. The prophet Isaiah predicted the coming of a messiah, a good and powerful leader for Israel. Christians believe that the messiah was Jesus.

In Islam, the great prophet is Muhammad, the founder of Islam. Muslims also follow the teachings of some Hebrew prophets, such as Moses.

See also **Moses; Jesus;** and **Muhammad.**

protein

Protein is one of the substances your body needs to grow and work properly. These substances are called *nutrients.* The other nutrients your body needs are carbohydrates, fats, vitamins, minerals, and water. Almost all foods contain some protein. Some foods—such as eggs, milk, cheese, fish, meat, beans, and nuts—are high in protein.

Your body needs protein every day to carry on its activities. Protein is used to build new body tissues and to repair worn-out ones. Every cell in your body contains protein. Protein is part of the muscles, bones, skin, and blood. The protein in muscles

Proteins come from dairy products, eggs, fish, meat, and nuts.

allows them to *contract*—tighten. The protein in bones and teeth provides their rigid framework. The protein in hair, nails, and skin forms a protective coating for the body. Protein also carries oxygen and nutrients in the blood.

There are thousands of kinds of proteins. All proteins are large chemicals made of building blocks called *amino acids.* The amino acids are strung together like the beads of a necklace. There are 22 different amino acids, and each kind of protein has its own arrangement and number of them. Many proteins contain 100 to 300 amino acids. Most proteins are bent and twisted into various shapes. A few proteins are straight strings of amino acids.

When you eat foods containing protein, digestive juices in your stomach and small intestine break them apart into individual amino acids. These are absorbed into the blood and carried to cells throughout the body. Each cell puts the amino acids together to form the proteins it needs. Sometimes the cells also take apart the amino acids and construct new amino acids from the parts.

Of the 20 amino acids, the body can put together all but eight. The eight that the body cannot make are called *essential amino acids.* In general, foods from plants do not contain all eight of the essential amino acids. If you eat only vegetables, you should combine grains and beans to get all the amino acids you need.

See also **nutrition.**

Protestant churches

Protestants are Christians whose churches trace some of their beliefs to the Protestant Reformation. This was a religious movement that began in Europe in the 1500s. It caused people to leave the old Christian church of Europe and form new churches. The original Christian church is known today as the Roman Catholic Church. (*See* **Reformation.**)

Baptists, Methodists, Lutherans, and Presbyterians are among the largest Protestant groups in North America. Over 350 million people in the world today belong to Protestant churches.

The earliest Protestant churches grew from the work of Martin Luther and John Calvin. Luther was a monk and teacher in Germany who wanted *reforms*—changes—in the church. The leaders of the Catholic church did not agree with Luther and refused to make the changes he wanted. He and his followers formed a new church, which we know today as the Lutheran church. (*See* **Luther, Martin.**)

John Calvin lived and taught in Switzerland. His followers began the Reformed church in the Netherlands and the Presbyterian church in Scotland. At about the same time, the Church of England separated from the Catholic church. The Church of England is also called the Anglican church in England, and the Episcopal church in the United States.

The United States has a very rich Protestant history. The New England colonies were founded by Puritans. The Puritans followed the teachings of John Calvin and were driven out of the Church of England. The Congregational and Unitarian churches grew out of the churches founded by the Puritans. (*See* **Puritans.**)

The early Baptist churches followed the teachings of several early reformers, but grew very slowly in Europe. In the United States, Baptist churches grew rapidly. Today, the Baptists make up the largest Protestant group.

A simple cross like this one stands in many Protestant churches.

Methodism started in England in the 1700s. A clergyman of the Church of England, John Wesley, wanted reforms in his church. He had such a strict, regular method of following his religion that people began to call him a "methodist." Methodism spread to the United States, where it grew rapidly. In the early 1800s, Methodist ministers rode out on horseback to bring Christian teachings to pioneers in the West. Today, Methodists are the second-largest Protestant group in the United States.

Protestants believe that an individual can reach God directly, without special rituals. A person receives God's blessing when he or she has faith. Protestants consider the Bible the center of their religion. In general, their worship is simpler than worship in Roman Catholic churches.

See also **Christianity.**

LARGE PROTESTANT CHURCH GROUPS IN THE U.S.	
Family	Members
Baptists	30,000,000
Methodists	15,500,000
Lutherans	8,500,000
Pentecostal Churches	8,000,000
Presbyterian/Reformed Churches	6,500,000
Churches of Christ	4,000,000
Episcopalians	2,500,000

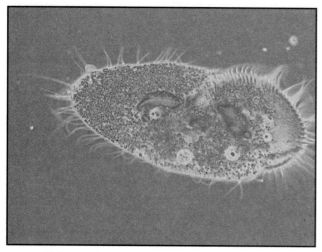

This protozoan is a *ciliate*. It moves when its tiny cilia beat together.

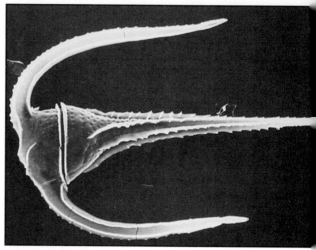

Dinoflagellates are tiny protists. Billions of them live in seawater.

protist

Protists form one of the kingdoms of living things—as do monerans, fungi, plants, and animals. Most of the living things in the protist kingdom are only a single cell and are too small to see without a microscope. Bacteria, protozoans, and some algae are among the protists. (*See* **bacteria; protozoan;** and **algae.**)

All protists live where it is moist. Many of them live in oceans, rivers, and ponds. Some live in moist soil. Most protists reproduce by *mitosis*—one cell dividing into two cells.

Most protists can move from place to place. Many kinds have hairlike structures called *cilia* sticking out from the cell. The cilia beat together and move the protist through water. The paramecium is a protist that moves this way. Other protists, such as amebas, move by stretching out *pseudopods* —false feet. The rest of the cell flows into the pseudopod. (*See* **ameba.**)

Protists get food in various ways. Some protists are hunters—they chase and capture their food. Some protists have tiny dart-like weapons to help them capture their food. Other protists, including some kinds of algae, make their own food by photosynthesis, the way plants do. Still other protists, such as euglenas, do both. Euglenas can move swiftly through the water to catch prey. When no food is available, they use photosynthesis. (*See* **photosynthesis.**)

protozoan

Protozoans are complex one-celled living things. They are members of the protist kingdom. They live nearly everywhere on earth, in water and moist soil. Protozoans are protists that feed on other living things. (*See* **protist.**)

Protozoans are divided into four groups according to the way they move. Members of the *flagellates* have a long thread called a *flagellum* at one end of the cell. The flagellum whips back and forth, moving the protozoan through the water. One kind of flagellate causes a serious illness called African sleeping sickness.

The *ciliates* have short threads called *cilia* sticking out all around the cell. The cilia beat together and move these protozoans. Ciliates chase down their food. One ciliate is the paramecium. Many students have looked at a paramecium under a microscope.

Protozoans in the *sarcodine* group move by changing their shapes. Part of the cell flows forward, then the rest of the cell follows. The flowing part of the cell is called a *psuedopod*—a false foot. The ameba is the best-known sarcodine. It changes shape not only to move but also to capture food by surrounding it. (*See* **ameba.**)

Radiolarians and *foraminiferans* are sarcodines that form hard shells. Under a microscope, these shells appear delicate and complex. Billions and billions of these shells

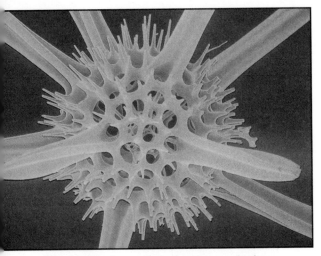

The shell of a radiolarian has a design that is like the design of a snowflake.

have fallen to the ocean floor, forming chalky deposits. The White Cliffs of Dover in England are made of these deposits.

The fourth group of protozoans—the *sporozoans*—do not have a special way to move. All of the sporozoans are parasites. The disease malaria is caused by a sporozoan.

Almost all protozoans reproduce *asexually*—a single protozoan is the parent of two or more offspring. For example, amebas divide in two. Paramecia, however, reproduce *sexually*. Two paramecia produce offspring together. (*See* **reproduction**.)

Protozoans are important links in food chains in the ocean. They are food for other protists and small animals, which in turn become food for others. (*See* **food chain**.)

psychiatry

Psychiatry is the branch of medicine concerned with how the mind and body work together. Some physical illnesses are triggered by mental stress. People with mental problems often feel tired or physically ill. A doctor who specializes in psychiatry is called a *psychiatrist*.

Some people have problems that make it difficult for them to get along with people and to live satisfying lives. For example, they may be so afraid of people that they cannot leave their own house. They may hear imaginary voices. They may feel that they cannot always control what they say or do.

Psychiatrists use treatments called *therapies* to help people overcome their problems. Talk therapy involves a series of discussions between the psychiatrist and one or more patients. Some therapies involve doing physical exercises. A kind of therapy called *psychoanalysis* was first developed by Sigmund Freud. (*See* **Freud, Sigmund**.)

Some people are treated with drugs that change how they feel and behave. For example, a violent person may take certain drugs to be able to lead a safer and calmer life.

See also **psychology**.

psychology

Psychology (SY-kah-leh-gee) is the study of human behavior and feelings. *Psychologists*—scientists who study psychology—are interested in what makes people angry, violent, shy, or kind. They want to know what makes people feel happy or sad. They study how people learn and reason. They wonder what dreams can tell us. They are interested in how people in families and in other groups get along with each other.

Scientists called *psychiatrists* study many of the same things as psychologists. But psychiatrists study how the mind and body work together. They are medical doctors and work in a field of medicine called *psychiatry*. (*See* **psychiatry**.)

Psychologists do research to find answers to their questions. They conduct scientific experiments to test their *hypotheses*—ideas. They observe and interview people and take notes on what they see and hear. They do this to find patterns in how people behave.

Psychologists use their knowledge to help people live more happily. When people have worries that do not go away, or have trouble getting along with other people, they may decide to talk with a psychologist. The psychologist helps them understand what to do about their problems. The results of psychological studies also suggest ways for people to change bad habits and to improve their ability to learn.

Learning, memory, thinking, emotions, and personality are only five of the areas of behavior studied by psychologists.

Learning A newborn baby cannot walk, talk, or dress himself or herself. Yet within the first few years of life, a child can learn to do all this and more. What enables a person to learn these skills and others, such as playing sports or a musical instrument? Studies by psychologists have found that people learn things in different ways. In many cases, people learn how to behave by being punished or rewarded for what they have done. (*See* **learning**.)

Memory A person's memory is his or her ability to recall something that was learned or experienced in the past. Psychologists have found that there are stages of memory. First, you have *sensory perception.* This means that you see, hear, taste, smell, or touch something. Next, what you sensed enters *short-term memory.* Here, the information is held for as long as you are thinking about it. You use short-term memory when you look up a telephone number and then dial it without writing it down. Minutes after

Psychology studies how we use our senses. This boy is trying to do a puzzle by feel.

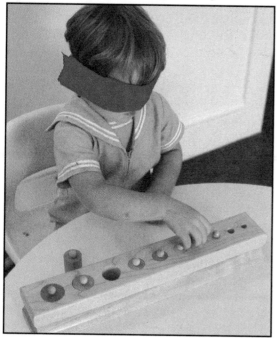

Psychologists can often help people who are depressed or anxious.

the call is made, you have probably forgotten the phone number.

Long-term memory, on the other hand, is a permanent storehouse for information. Birthdays, names, the words of a favorite song, and past experiences are kept in long-term memory. People shift things from short-term to long-term memory as needed. Often, people's memories are *selective.* This means that they tend to remember certain experiences longer and more clearly than some other experiences. (*See* **memory**.)

Thinking Psychologists are interested in how people *reason*—how they think out their problems and try to solve them. Psychologists believe that as children grow older, their ability to reason improves. For example, if a young child is served spinach in a small pile at mealtime, the child is likely to think there is not very much of it to eat. By age six or seven, the child knows that the amount is the same whether it is pushed together or spread out.

Psychologists call a person's ability to learn, to reason, and to understand things *intelligence.* There are several tests that try to measure a person's intelligence. This measurement is called an *intelligence quotient—IQ.* (*See* **intelligence**.)

Emotions Emotions are feelings—such as happiness, sadness, fear, love, and hate. A person's smiles or tears are a kind of "language" for expressing his or her emotions. This language is the same for people all over the world.

Above, family members and friends love and need each other, but they also get into arguments and can hurt each other. Psychologists study how people get along together. Below, an animal experiment helps a psychologist study one kind of learning.

Your emotions and your physical state are closely related. For example, when you feel frightened, your heart beats faster, you take fast, short breaths, and your blood races from your stomach to your brain, heart, and muscles. The fear makes your body prepare to either fight or run away from the danger that is making you afraid.

Personality One of the mysteries of human life is personality—all the ways of thinking and feeling that make each person special. Psychologists believe that people are born with some of the things that make up their personalities. They also feel that personality is shaped by a person's surroundings and experiences. For example, some children seem to be born shy. Their parents can encourage them to be less timid, but they cannot force them to be bold.

Puerto Rico

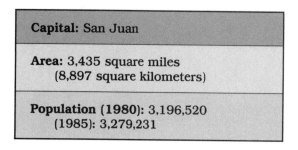

Capital: San Juan
Area: 3,435 square miles (8,897 square kilometers)
Population (1980): 3,196,520 (1985): 3,279,231

The people of Puerto Rico are citizens of the United States, yet Puerto Rico is not a state. It is a partly independent island under the protection of the United States.

Land Puerto Rico is an island in the West Indies island group, about 1,000 miles (1,610 kilometers) southeast of Florida. The Atlantic Ocean is to the north of Puerto Rico, and the Caribbean Sea is to its south.

Puerto Rico has miles of beautiful, sandy beaches dotted with palm trees. Inland, hills are covered by dense rain forests. The hills come together to form a range of rugged mountains running east to west across the island. The highest peak is 4,400 feet (1,341 meters) above sea level.

Puerto Rico's climate is mild all year long. Winds called *trade winds* blow constantly from the northeast, keeping temperatures comfortable. Hurricanes can hit the island between June and November. They cause violent rainstorms and heavy damage.

History Puerto Rico was discovered by Christopher Columbus in 1493, on his second voyage to the New World. In 1509, Juan Ponce de Léon claimed the island for Spain.

The Spaniards began growing sugarcane on the island in 1515. Three years later, they brought in African slaves to work on the plantations. Few Spaniards wanted to live in Puerto Rico because it had little gold or silver. For centuries, the population was small, and almost all of the people were poor.

Still, Puerto Rico was an important part of the Spanish Empire, for it was the West Indian island closest to Spain. A large fort was built at San Juan, the capital, because other European countries wanted the island.

The United States took control of Puerto Rico in 1898, when Spain lost the Spanish-American War. Puerto Ricans became U.S. citizens in 1917. They were ruled by a governor from the mainland United States until 1948. Since then, Puerto Ricans have elected their own governor and lawmaking body.

Puerto Rico and the United States still have strong ties. The U.S. military defends the island, and Puerto Rico receives money

A colorful fire station in the city of Ponce (below). At right, Boy Scouts on an outing.

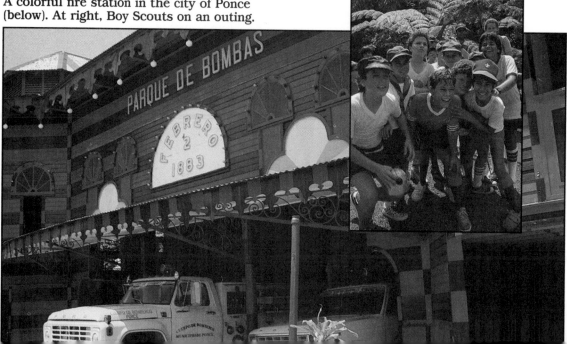

from the U.S. government. Puerto Ricans do not pay federal taxes, cannot vote in U.S. elections, and have no voting representative in the U.S. Congress. Puerto Rican men may be required to serve in the U.S. military.

Poverty has always been a problem in Puerto Rico. The economy was based mainly on farming until the late 1940s. Then Puerto Ricans decided to develop modern factories. The factories produced a variety of goods and provided jobs for thousands of people. As a result, Puerto Rico now has a higher income per person than any other place in Latin America.

People When the Spaniards came to Puerto Rico, they found Taino Indians living there. Over the next 75 years, most of the Indians died of disease or were killed, but some hid in the mountains. Today, almost all Puerto Ricans are of Spanish descent. Some people have Indian and black ancestry.

The population of Puerto Rico is very large compared to the island's size. In fact, if Puerto Rico were a state, it would rank second in the number of people per square mile and forty-eighth in size!

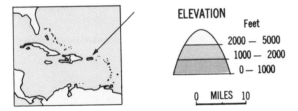

ELEVATION
Feet
2000 — 5000
1000 — 2000
0 — 1000

0   MILES   10

Spanish-style farm towns and villages dot the island. Agriculture is still important to the island's economy. Sugarcane is grown on the coastal plains. Some of it is made into rum. Other crops include coffee, bananas, pineapple, tobacco, and citrus fruits. Cattle, hogs, and poultry are raised.

Many people moved from the countryside to the cities to work in Puerto Rico's factories. They produce medicines and drugs, chemicals, machinery, food products, clothing, and many other items.

San Juan, on the northern shore, is the political, industrial, commercial, and cultural center of the island. It has old Spanish buildings and tall modern ones. Many people live in large housing developments. Those less fortunate are crowded into slums. Beaches and luxury hotels near San Juan attract more than 1 million tourists a year.

Ponce, on the southern coast, is the island's second-largest city. It is an important seaport, famous for its Spanish architecture and for its art museum.

Mayagüez, in western Puerto Rico, is the island's third-largest city. It is an agricultural center.

Many Puerto Ricans have become famous as musicians, athletes, or actors. Among them are Jose Feliciano, Roberto Clemente, Orlando Cepeda, Jose Ferrer, and Rita Moreno. Cellist Pablo Casals lived in Puerto Rico for many years.

pulsar

A pulsar is a spinning object in outer space that sends out radio signals in regular, frequent *pulses*—flashes. Pulsars may also send out other kinds of signals, such as X rays or gamma rays. But the on-off pulsing signal is a pulsar's special feature.

When pulsars were first discovered, in 1967, some people thought the pulses were messages being sent by creatures from outer space. Within weeks, however, astronomers figured out that the signals were coming from objects.

In some ways, a pulsar's signal is like the light from lighthouse. In a lighthouse, a lamp rotates and sends out a light beam that sweeps around in a circle. The lamp is always on but it appears to flash off and on. When the light is pointing away from you, you do not see it. A pulsar's radio signal, like a lighthouse light, is on all the time. The signal comes from one part of the pulsar. As the pulsar rotates, the radio beam sweeps around in a circle. To us on earth, the signal seems to flash on and off.

pump

Water runs downhill. A river flows down the mountains to a valley. Water stored in a tank on the roof will run down through pipes into the building. But what do we do when we have to move water or other liquids from a low place to a high place? How do we lift water or oil from a deep well, or gasoline from an underground tank? We do these things by using a pump, a device that lifts liquids.

A simple kind of pump is the *lift pump*. This type of pump is used to get water from a well by hand. The pump is aboveground, and a long pipe leads down from it to the well water, which is underground. As you move the pump handle up and down, a partial vacuum is produced in the pump. Water is pushed up from the well by air pressure. Using a hand pump is hard work. But it is easier than bringing up a heavy bucket of water with a rope. Today, most wells have electric pumps. A powerful electric motor provides the power that creates the vacuum that draws the water.

The bicycle pump is an example of a pump that moves gases. People use this simple device to pump air into bicycle tires, rubber rafts, and footballs.

An electric pump called a *compressor* moves a gas through tubes in refrigerators and air conditioners.

An electric fan is a kind of pump, too. The swirling blades of the fan move air from one place to another.

1. When you push the pump handle down, water is sucked upward. 2. When you pull up, some water is trapped. 3. When you push down again, it is forced out of the spout.

vacuum

These Muppets, created by Jim Henson (second from left), are hand and rod puppets. Puppeteers use their hands to operate the puppets' heads. They move the puppets' hands with rods.

pumpkin

A pumpkin is a large, orange-colored fruit that grows on vines and has large, prickly leaves. The pumpkin has a hard outer covering called a *rind*. Its inside is soft, stringy, and has many seeds.

Squashes and pumpkins are closely related, but squashes come in many different shapes and colors. The large winter squash grows on a vine, and tastes something like a pumpkin. Many people call it a pumpkin by mistake.

The pumpkin is a source of vitamins A and C. People eat pumpkins mainly as pies, but also in puddings, soups, cakes, and breads. Toasted pumpkin seeds are a popular snack food.

Every year in the United States, millions of pumpkins are made into *jack-o'-lanterns* for Halloween. You and your parents can make a jack-o'-lantern by cutting the top off a pumpkin and scooping out the inside. Then you carve or paint a face on the outside. If a lighted candle is placed inside the jack-o'-lantern, the face will glow in the dark. (*See* **Halloween.**)

Pumpkins are among the oldest foods found in North America. Indians grew and ate them for thousands of years before the first Europeans arrived.

puppet

A puppet is a doll-like figure that can be made to perform for an audience. Puppets can be of people, animals, or imaginary creatures. They are controlled by one or more people, called *puppeteers*. Most puppeteers work hidden behind a puppet stage.

There are many kinds of puppets. A *hand puppet* has a loose costume that slips over the puppeteer's hand. The puppeteer puts the middle finger in the head and the thumb and the little finger inside the puppet's arms. Moving the fingers makes the puppet's head and arms move.

A *marionette,* also called a *string puppet* is more complicated. It has a hard body that bends at the joints. Strings or wires are attached to the body. The other ends of the strings or wires are fastened to a control piece made of wood. The puppeteer stands above the stage and moves the puppet by tilting the piece of wood and by pulling the strings. This makes the marionette walk, wave, turn, bend, and even dance.

Rod puppets are controlled by sticks from below. In Japan, rod puppets as large as children are used in a kind of performance called *Bunraku*. A Bunraku puppet is operated by several puppeteers who can be seen by the audience.

Puritans

The Puritans were English Protestants. They helped settle the New England area of North America during the 1600s.

In the late 1500s, some English people disagreed with the practices of the Church of England. They believed worship should be based on personal prayer, preaching, and reading from the Bible. They wanted to rid churches of statues and stained-glass windows. Their desire to "purify" the Church of England earned them the name Puritans. When their efforts failed, they decided to separate from the Church of England.

One group of these *Separatists* crossed the Atlantic Ocean in 1620 and founded Plymouth Colony in Massachusetts. They became known as the Pilgrims. In 1628, another group of Puritans landed at Salem, Massachusetts, and started the Massachusetts Bay Colony. Puritan settlements were soon set up all along the coast of Massachusetts. In 1630, John Winthrop, the governor of the Massachusetts Bay Colony, led about 1,000 Puritans north to start the city of Boston. The first laws for the Massachusetts Bay Colony, written in 1641, required everyone to follow Puritan laws and ideas.

See also **Pilgrims** and **Plymouth.**

puzzle

A puzzle is a kind of game in which a person must solve a problem, find an answer, or put something together. There are many kinds of puzzles. For some people, working on puzzles is an interesting hobby. Puzzles are also used in schools to help children learn.

A *jigsaw* puzzle is a picture or design on cardboard or wood that has been cut into odd-shaped flat pieces. To solve the puzzle, you must fit all the pieces together. The simplest jigsaw puzzles have only a few pieces. The most complicated ones may have 2,000 pieces or more.

A three-dimensional jigsaw puzzle uses solid shapes instead of flat shapes. The

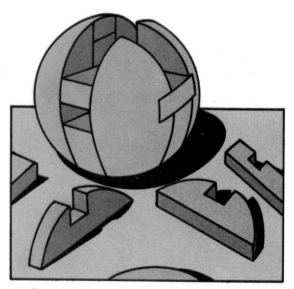

Solid puzzles made of wood or metal are popular with children and grown-ups.

solid shapes fit together to make objects such as cubes or balls. Some shapes will not fit unless certain other shapes are already in place.

In another kind of picture puzzle, the picture reveals itself when you connect numbered dots. One kind of picture puzzle uses a complex drawing. Hidden in the drawing are odd things in wrong places—such as a fish in a tree. You can spot the things by carefully looking over the puzzle.

In a maze, many winding paths are drawn on a sheet of paper. But once you begin to follow them, you find that most of them come to a dead end. You must find the one path that leads to your goal.

Some puzzles involve words. One simple kind of word puzzle is a *riddle*. A riddle is a clever question. To solve the riddle, you just need to find the right answer. Often, the answer to the riddle depends on a *pun*—a word with more than one meaning.

A Famous Riddle

As I was going to St. Ives, I met a man with seven wives.

Every wife had seven bags, every bag had seven cats, every cat had seven kits;

Kits, cats, bags, wives, how many were going to St. Ives?

Answer: Only one. I was going to St. Ives; the others were going in the other direction — leaving St. Ives.

Animal Antics

The starred (*) words in this puzzle have to do with animals.

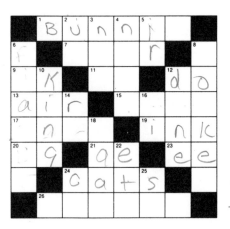

Across

* **1.** Easter animal.
* **7.** Fawns, does, and bucks.
* **9.** Everything but the kitchen si _ _ .
* **11.** Famous television horse, Mr. _ _ .
* **12.** The opposite of *don't*.
* **13.** What we breathe.
* **15.** The Ugly Duckling became this.
* **17.** Part of a door.
* **19.** Liquid inside a pen.
* **20.** A,B,C,D, _ , F, _ .
* **21.** Two vowels.
* **23.** Ducks have big f _ _ t.
* **24.** Grown-up kittens.
* **26.** These race in the Kentucky Derby.

Down

* **2.** Abbreviation of *advertisement*.
* **3.** This lives in a hive.
* **4.** Flowers sleep here.
* **5.** The letters that turn *the* into *their*.
* **6.** These move along the ground without legs.
* **8.** Mule.
* **10.** He is married to the queen.
* **12.** A large dog: Great _ _ .
* **14.** A mouse is a _ _ dent.
* **16.** Postal abbreviation of *Wisconsin*.
* **18.** Her babies are called cubs.
* **22.** Contraction for *it is*.
* **24.** Abbreviation of *company*.
* **25.** Abbreviation of *southeast*.

In a crossword (above), the player fills in words based on clues.
In a maze (below left), the player must find a way from the start to the finish.
In a magic square (below right), the numbers 1 through 9 are arranged in a square
so that they add to the same sum across, down, and from corner to corner.

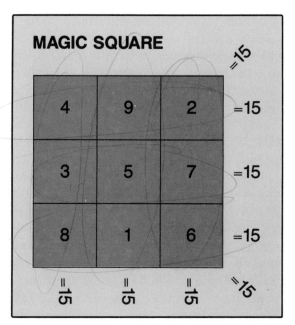

One of the most popular word puzzles is the *crossword puzzle*. A crossword puzzle has many small squares that will be filled with the letters of words. The puzzle maker provides clues for the words. Some words are spelled running across the puzzle. Others are spelled running down. Many letters must fit both an "across" word and a "down" word.

Another kind of word puzzle is a *cryptogram*. This is a message in code. The solver must find a way to break the code and read the message. (*See* **codes and ciphers**.)

There are many kinds of puzzles that use numbers. Solving a number puzzle may depend on using simple reasoning or on doing simple arithmetic. One famous number puzzle is the "magic square."

An Egyptian pyramid is a giant tomb. Thousands of years ago, a king was buried in a small chamber deep under the pyramid. The chamber was reached by a long tunnel.

pyramid

A pyramid is a building with a square base and four sides shaped like triangles. The sides come together to form a point at the top. In ancient times, pyramids were often used as religious temples. Ruins of pyramids built by the Maya and Aztec still exist in the Americas today. The most famous pyramids, however, are those built over 4,500 years ago in Egypt.

These pyramids were tombs—burial places—built for Egyptian kings, who were known as *pharaohs*. The Egyptians believed in a life after death. They felt that people needed their earthly bodies in order to live this new life. For that reason, they preserved dead bodies as *mummies* and buried them with objects that were used in everyday life. Since the pharaohs were the most important people in ancient Egypt, their tombs were filled with gold, jewels, and other treasures. (*See* **mummy**.)

There are about 70 known pyramids along Egypt's Nile River. The pyramids are made of rough stone blocks or mud bricks. A layer of limestone was added to give the buildings a smooth, finished look. Scientists believe that it took thousands of Egyptian peasants well over ten years to build each pyramid. The peasants dragged blocks of heavy stone along sloping earthen ramps and slid the blocks into place. The ramps were removed after the pyramids were completed.

Each pyramid had an entrance in its north wall. From there, a narrow passageway led to a room called a *chamber*. The chamber was carved out of rock and contained the pharaoh's mummy and possessions. Sometimes, a smaller pyramid was built for the queen alongside the pharaoh's pyramid.

The three pyramids at Giza are the largest Egyptian pyramids standing today. Giza is on the Nile River, south of Cairo, the Egyptian capital. The biggest of these, the Great Pyramid, was built for the Egyptian pharaoh Khufu, also known as Cheops, about 2600 B.C. The Great Pyramid covers about 13 acres (5.2 hectares) of land. Its sides are 756 feet (226 meters) long. The top is 450 feet (135 meters) high—as tall as a 40-story skyscraper. It is made of sandstone.

Thieves broke into many of the pyramids and stole gold, jewels, and other objects. Because of this, later Egyptian pharaohs hid their tombs in the walls of cliffs along the Nile River. This area is known as the *Valley of the Kings*.

The Semites borrowed the Egyptian symbol for "monkey," calling it *qoph*, their word for "monkey."

The Phoenicians used a symbol of a knotted cord when they wrote the letter *qoph*.

Around the year 114, the Romans gave the letter the form it still has today.

Quakers

A Quaker is a Christian who belongs to the Religious Society of Friends. This group was founded in England around the year 1650 by a preacher named George Fox. "Friends" is another name by which Quakers are known.

Quakers teach that God guides all people, Christian or otherwise, by an "inner light." This is one reason why Quakers respect and value every person.

Quakers are also *pacifists*—they believe it is wrong to use violence to settle arguments. For this reason, Quakers do not become soldiers. Instead, they perform other kinds of

Quakers of the 1800s dressed in simple gray or black clothing.

service in wartime, such as working as doctors or teachers. They have also defended men and women of all faiths who share the belief that violence and war are wrong.

Quakers worship in *meeting houses.* During their meetings, they sit together in silence and speak only when they believe they have a message God has given them to share.

Quakers have played an important part in the history of the United States. In 1682, the Quaker William Penn founded the colony of Pennsylvania. He also planned its capital city and named it Philadelphia, a Greek word meaning "brotherly love." Penn and the Quakers welcomed people of all religions to Philadelphia. By 1710, it had become the largest city in the American colonies. (*See* **Penn, William.**)

Many Quakers were among the first people in the American colonies to speak out against slavery. Anthony Benezet and John Woolman were two Quakers who helped lead this struggle. They worked hard to persuade fellow Christians to free their slaves. Woolman traveled throughout the South and talked to slave owners about the evils of owning slaves. Benezet helped to persuade the British Parliament to outlaw slavery. He also opened a school for black children in his home in Philadephia.

In 1833, another Quaker, Lucretia Mott, helped organize the American Anti-Slavery Society and the Philadelphia Female Anti-Slavery Society. Mott and Susan B. Anthony, also a Quaker, worked hard for women's rights. (*See* **Anthony, Susan B.**)

Most of today's Quakers live in the United States. Smaller groups of Quakers live in England and other countries.

quarry

A quarry is an open hole dug into a large deposit of rock in the earth. The rock is cut into blocks, so it can be removed and used for building. As more rock is taken out, the hole gets deeper and larger. After all the usable rock has been removed, the quarry is abandoned. Marble, limestone, sandstone, slate, and granite are a few of the kinds of rocks that are taken from quarries.

Our ancestors used the loose rocks they found on the ground to make points and

Workers in this huge granite quarry seem as small as insects.

blades for their tools and weapons. When people began to build large stone structures, they needed blocks of stone larger than what they could find near the surface. They began digging for large rocks.

The Egyptians were building with limestone and granite blocks at least 5,000 years ago. They got the stones from quarries and used them to build pyramids, temples, and cities. Many of the blocks were huge and weighed more than 1,800 kilograms (2 tons) each.

Over millions of years, rock on the surface of the earth has been broken down into soil, sand, and smaller rocks. Below the earth's surface are huge deposits of solid rock that have not been broken up by the forces of nature. These rock deposits are sometimes called *formations*. Each kind of rock has a different kind of formation, so each kind of rock is *quarried*—dug and removed—in a different way.

Granite is an *igneous* rock. Igneous rock was formed millions of years ago, when melted rock cooled. It is very hard and is quarried by drilling and blasting out huge slabs.

Marble and slate are two kinds of *metamorphic* rock. Metamorphic rock is not as old as igneous rock. It was formed by the earth's heat and pressure and is quite hard. Marble and slate are usually cut from the earth rather than blasted.

Sandstone and limestone are called *sedimentary* or *stratified* rock. Rock of this kind is not as old as igneous or metamorphic rock. Sedimentary rock is formed from animal shells and bones, and layers of sand. It is softer than other kinds of rock, so it is the easiest to cut.

Digging, cutting, and hauling stone from quarries used to be done by animals and people. Today, the heavy lifting and hauling is done by powerful machinery. High-speed saws and drills, with cutting edges of hard steel and industrial diamonds, cut through tons of rock.

See also **rock.**

blue quartz

amethyst

citrine   smoky quartz

Quartz crystals have many colors and sizes.

quartz

Quartz is a mineral made of silicon and oxygen—the two most common elements in the earth's crust. This helps to explain why there is so much quartz.

Beach sand and desert sand are mostly tiny grains of quartz. Many of the rocks that form mountains are full of quartz. In mountains made of granite, the granite is quartz mixed with the mineral feldspar. In mountains made of sandstone, the quartz is like grains of cemented beach sand.

Quartz is also a crystal. The atoms in a crystal always arrange themselves in a particular way that gives the mineral its special shape. A quartz crystal has flat, smooth sides, and sharp edges going up the length of the crystal. A quartz crystal often comes to a point, like a pyramid. (*See* **crystal.**)

Quartz crystals come in different sizes and colors. Some are tiny grains, and some are 3 to 6 meters (10 to 20 feet) long. Quartz may be clear like glass, or white and cloudy. Purple quartz, called *amethyst,* dark brown *smoky quartz,* and pink *rosy quartz* are used as gems. Quartz crystals are also used in radio transmitters, watches, clocks, lenses, and building materials.

See also **mineral; rock;** and **sand.**

quasar

A quasar is one of the most mysterious objects in outer space. It looks like a small, faint star, but it is very powerful. Some quasars give off about 1,000 times as much energy as a whole galaxy—100 trillion times as much energy as the sun! Besides light, some quasars also give off radio signals. Quasars are the most distant objects we have observed in the universe. Astronomers think that the quasars farthest from Earth may be 12 million *light-years* away. This means it would take you 12 million years to reach them if you were traveling at the speed of light.

Astronomers wonder what makes a quasar so powerful. Some believe a giant black hole is at the center of a quasar. The gravity of a black hole is so strong that it sucks in light as well as matter. As the black hole in a quasar draws in stars, dust clouds, and other matter, it somehow gives energy to everything in the surrounding area, making it glow. Other astronomers think that quasars are not so far away or that powerful, but are just small, faint stars. (*See* **black hole.**)

Astronomers discovered quasars in 1960 by using the Hale telescope near San Diego, California. Today, more than 1,000 quasars have been found, all of them at the farthest reaches of the universe.

An X-ray photo of quasar 3C273. Light colors show areas of high X-ray energy.

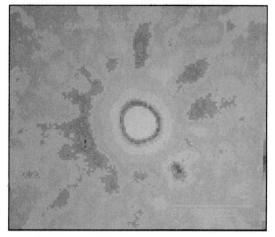

Quebec

Capital: Quebec City
Area: 594,860 square miles (1,540,687 square kilometers) (largest province)
Population (1981): 6,438,403 (1985): about 6,562,200 (2nd-largest province)
Became a province: July 1, 1867 (one of four original provinces)

Quebec is the largest of Canada's ten provinces. It lies in the eastern part of the country, and has more people than any other province except Ontario. About four-fifths of Quebec's people are descended from French settlers. This makes Quebec the only province where the majority of people follow French customs instead of British ones.

Land Much of the province is surrounded by water. Hudson Bay lies to the west and north. The Gulf of St. Lawrence and the St. Lawrence River cut through the southern part of Quebec. (*See* **St. Lawrence River.**)

A narrow plain with rich soil lies on both sides of the St. Lawrence River. On the plain, summers are mild, and winters are cold and snowy. Most of the province's farms are here. The majority of Quebec's people live in the cities and towns in this area.

North of the St. Lawrence Plain is the Canadian Shield. This is a chain of ancient mountains with many lakes and rushing rivers. The southern part of the shield is covered with forests. Few plants can grow in the bitter cold of Quebec's far north.

Large mineral deposits are among Quebec's greatest natural resources. Most of the province's iron ore and copper is found in the Canadian Shield region. Some of the largest asbestos mines in the world are in southeastern Quebec. Marble, nickel, granite, and lead are also mined.

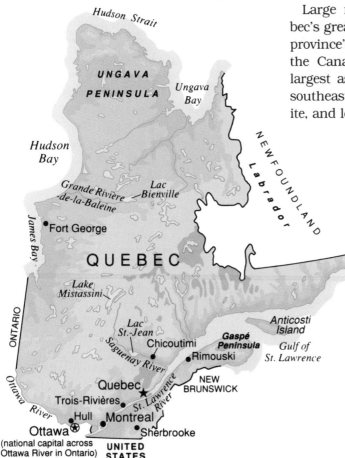

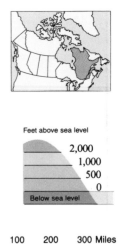

Feet above sea level

2,000
1,000
500
0
Below sea level

0   100   200   300 Miles

0   100 200 300 Kilometers

There are power plants along many of Quebec's rivers. These plants produce great amounts of electricity. In fact, Quebec is the main supplier of hydroelectricity in Canada. Quebec also has more forests than any other Canadian province. Trees are cut and sent to the province's pulp and paper mills. Quebec leads the rest of Canada in the production of *newsprint*—the paper on which newspapers are printed.

People Almost all of Quebec's people are French Canadians. The rest are of British, Indian, or Eskimo descent. Most of the people speak French and follow the Roman Catholic faith. Many French Canadians feel that English-speaking Canadians have too much power in Canada. They would like Quebec to become an independent country. This worries Canada's government, which wants the country to stay united.

Montreal is the largest city in Quebec and has more people than any other city in Canada. It is also the world's second-largest French-speaking city, after Paris, France.

The city lies on an island in the St. Lawrence River. (*See* **Montreal**.)

Quebec City is the capital of the province. It is Canada's oldest city, and its French atmosphere has made it a popular center of tourism.

History The Indians and the Eskimo were the first peoples to live in the area that is now Quebec Province. The French explorer Jacques Cartier came to Quebec in 1534. Another Frenchman, Samuel de Champlain, founded the first settlement, at Quebec City in 1608. By 1763, there were about 65,000 French Canadians living in the province. That same year, France gave Quebec to Great Britain after losing the French and Indian War. The British ruled the province until Canada became a nation in 1867. (*See* **Cartier, Jacques** and **French and Indian War.**)

---

queen, *see* **kings and queens; monarchy**

Quebec City, the capital of Quebec, is built on hills overlooking the broad St. Lawrence River. The tall building at right is the Chateau Frontenac, a hotel.

quicksand

Quicksand is very loose, very wet sand. Areas of deep quicksand are found in the deltas of some rivers and along some beaches. Quicksand may not look any different from solid ground, so animals and people sometimes step into it by mistake.

Quicksand forms where there is a strong underground current of water. The water, bubbling up from deep in the ground, pushes the sand grains apart. They become so loose that they flow like water.

Although you cannot stand on quicksand, you can float on it. In fact, you can float higher on quicksand than on water. This is because quicksand is much denser.

Stories are sometimes told about animals and people being sucked into quicksand and disappearing. But quicksand does not pull things down into it. An animal or person trying to get out may simply become exhausted and drown. If you are caught in quicksand, instead of struggling, the best thing to do is float on your back and slowly work your way over to solid ground.

Below, quilting a patchwork quilt on a frame. At right, a detail of the patchwork pattern Double Wedding Ring.

quilting

Quilting is the art of sewing layers of fabric together by hand or machine. It is often used to create bedcoverings called *quilts.* Quilts are often hung as decorations on walls, too.

Most quilts are made like a sandwich, with a decorative cloth top, a cloth backing, and a middle layer of thick, cottony filling called *batting.*

In America, quilts were first made just for warmth. Cloth was scarce, so scraps of old clothing were saved and sewn together to make warm bed quilts. But quilting quickly became a folk art. Women took pride in designing attractive quilts. They showed off their sewing skills with the tiny, even stitches that held the layers together.

There are two main kinds of quilts. *Patchwork* quilt tops are made of many small pieces of fabric joined edge to edge. *Appliqué* quilt tops have shapes sewn on top of a background fabric.

Often, quilters use a frame or hoop to hold the fabric sandwich firmly while it is being quilted. The quilting stitches that hold the layers together may form a separate design or may outline the shapes in the top pattern. Finally, the quilt edges are finished all around, usually with a long, narrow strip of cloth called *binding.*

Today, people collect quilts and show them as works of art. The most beautiful are shown in museums. But quilts are being made for their original purpose. We still use quilts as bedcoverings to keep us warm.

The letter *R* began about 3000 B.C. as the Egyptian word symbol for the human head.

By 600 B.C., the Greeks used a P-shaped letter. They called this letter *rho*.

About 700 years later, the Romans gave the capital letter *R* the shape it has today.

rabbit

The rabbit is a mammal that has a coat of soft fur, a short tail, and long ears. Its back legs are longer and stronger than its front legs. Rabbits do not walk or run—they hop or leap. They can move very quickly, zigzagging to avoid capture. This is important because rabbits have many enemies, including owls, hawks, foxes, coyotes, and people. Rabbits live all over the world.

Rabbits can hear very well. Their excellent sense of smell helps them to find food and detect enemies. When a rabbit twitches its nose, it is opening and closing its nostrils. Special cells inside the nostrils pick up scents in the air. The rabbit's big eyes are on the sides of its head. This helps the rabbit see objects behind and to the side.

The two front teeth are large and very sharp. These teeth never stop growing. The rabbit keeps them short by gnawing on plants. A deep slit in the center of the upper lip—called a *harelip*—lets the rabbit gnaw even when its mouth is closed. Rabbits eat grass, roots, bark, and other plant matter. They can cause a lot of damage to crops.

Most rabbits live in underground burrows. They dig the burrows with their front paws and kick away the loose soil with their back feet. Each burrow has several passages and more than one entrance. Sometimes, many burrows will be connected to form a *warren.* More than 60 rabbits may live in a warren.

Female rabbits line their nests with grass and fur. This is where the babies are born. The newborn rabbits have no fur. Their eyes are closed, and they cannot hear. The mother rabbit cares for her young for several weeks, until they can live on their own. Soon after, she may give birth to another litter of babies. She may have five or more litters in one season.

The snowshoe rabbit changes color from season to season.

Wild Rabbits

snowshoe rabbit (winter)

desert cottontail

snowshoe rabbit (summer)

Domesticated Rabbits

Belgian hare

Himalayan rabbit

This black-tailed jackrabbit's ears are
thin enough for sunlight to shine through.

The raccoon has caught a fish—
a welcome winter meal.

Rabbits are closely related to hares. Hares look very much like rabbits, but most hares are larger than rabbits and have longer ears. One very familiar hare is the *jackrabbit.* Hares do not burrow. They make nests in shallow holes in the ground. Their babies are born with fur and open eyes.

Tame rabbits make appealing pets. If kept indoors, they can be trained to use a litter tray like a house cat. But their constant gnawing on furniture, doors, and lamp cords can be a problem. It is best to keep them outdoors in a large cage called a *hutch.* Pet rabbits eat pellets, oats, wheat, and fresh fruits and vegetables. They need fresh water every day. People also raise rabbits for their meat.

raccoon

The raccoon is a mammal with long, grayish brown fur and a mask of black fur across its face. It has five to ten black rings on its bushy tail. It is about as big as a house cat, but looks larger because it has bigger legs and a bushier coat.

There are two main kinds of raccoons. The common raccoon is found in North America and in Central America. The crab-eating raccoon lives in South America and the lower part of Central America. Both kinds usually weigh between 2.2 and 6.6 kilograms (5 to 15 pounds). In places with cold winters, raccoons eat a lot in autumn. Then they crawl into their homes and sleep through most of the winter. They do not hibernate, however. On a warm winter day, they will sit outdoors in the sunshine.

The home of a raccoon is called a *den.* Most raccoons make their dens in hollow trees, usually near forest streams. They rest during the day and search for food at night. Their favorite foods are fish and frogs, which they scoop out of the water with their paws. But raccoons will eat almost anything.

Many raccoons live on farms and in suburban areas, where they can become pests. In their hunt for food, they tip over garbage cans and invade gardens. They especially enjoy ripe corn.

Raccoons are good climbers. They climb trees to escape from danger. But if they are cornered, they will fight. Their sharp claws can cause painful wounds.

Raccoons mate in late winter. About two months later, the female gives birth to three or four cubs. At birth, the cubs weigh only 57 grams (2 ounces). They are helpless and cannot see. Their mother takes good care of them. When the cubs are about ten weeks old, they begin to leave the den. They follow their mother as she travels about, learning how to find food and live on their own.

Raccoons are friendly, curious animals, always eager to explore and to pick up and examine objects. But raccoons do not make good pets. They can live as pets when they are very young, but they soon become adults and want to be free.

race

In the 1400s, the sailors from Europe who landed in West Africa had a big surprise. Until they landed, they had thought that all humans were white or brown. But they discovered that the people of West Africa were black. The blacks were also amazed to see the sailors. They had always believed that all humans were black.

Both whites and blacks thought people who were different must have some sickness. Some whites and blacks were afraid of each other. They thought that people of a different color could be gods or devils.

People who studied differences in human beings gradually formed a theory of *races.* This theory tried to explain all the ways people of different skin color were different. At first, the theory said that there were three races—white, black, and yellow (or Oriental). Then it was discovered that many people seemed to be in-between—having some qualities from at least two groups. Explaining who belonged to a certain race became more and more complicated.

At the same time, scientists were discovering that it was difficult to find clear differences among people of various skin colors. For example, people of different colors share the same blood types. If they grow up in the same place, they speak the same way and learn the same things. Although their skins may be different colors, there is no important difference under the skin.

Unfortunately, some people still believe that people of a different skin color or heritage are inferior—not as good as other people. This belief is called *racism.* In the 1930s and 1940s, the German government, led by Adolf Hitler, announced that Jews, blacks,

and others who were not Germans were inferior and evil. The government sent millions of Jews and others to death because of their race. (*See* **Hitler, Adolf.**)

In the United States, many whites once believed that black people were not as good as whites. Until the early 1800s, blacks were brought to America as slaves. Even after slavery was ended in the 1860s, black people were forced to live apart from whites. They could not receive the same education. Gradually, in the 1900s, black Americans began to gain equal rights and opportunities. (*See* **black Americans** and **civil rights.**)

radar and sonar

When a sound wave hits a solid object, it bounces back. You hear the bounced-back sound wave as an echo. People use echoes of radio waves and sound waves to learn about things they cannot see. (*See* **echo.**)

Radar uses radio waves sent into the air by a transmitter. Most of the waves continue in a straight line. Those that hit something solid bounce away. Some of them bounce back to where they began. There, they show up on a radar screen. The pattern of the returning waves tells the size and shape of the object they hit. The time it takes for the radar waves to come back tells how far away

Blips on this radar screen may be planes, rainstorms, or other kinds of interference.

the object is. The word *radar* is formed from the words *ra*dio *d*etection *a*nd *r*anging.

Radar was first developed in wartime to spot aircraft in the sky. Today, it is still used by the armed forces, but it is also used in airports to help planes land safely. People who study the weather use radar to learn about rainstorms, hurricanes, and even dangerous winds. Pilots and ships' captains use radar equipment when traveling through bad weather, fog, or darkness. Police officers use radar to detect speeding cars.

Sonar—from the words *s*ound *n*avigation *a*nd *r*anging—uses sound waves to find things underwater. The sound waves used in sonar are very loud—millions of times stronger than your voice. They are sent from ships. Sonar can find submarines, shipwrecks, whales, and schools of fish. It is also used to measure the depth of the water and to map the seafloor.

radiation

Radiation is the movement of energy through space. Heat and light travel through space as radiation. So do radio waves. Other waves that radiate through space include microwaves, ultraviolet waves, X rays, and gamma rays. These waves are all forms of electromagnetic radiation.

We often use the word *radiation* to mean *ionizing radiation*—radiation that is powerful enough to knock electrons from an atom. High doses of ionizing radiation can damage or even kill living things, including humans.

Cosmic rays are a form of ionizing radiation that come from the sun and distant stars. Earth's atmosphere stops most cosmic rays from reaching the ground. Some elements in the earth's crust also produce strong radiation. They include radium and radon, a gas.

X rays are a form of strong radiation. They can pass through flesh, so they help doctors see into the body. But doctors use small doses of X rays, because too much can cause serious injury.

The materials used in nuclear power plants give off huge amounts of radiation. Workers in these plants must be protected from these materials. Wastes from the plants must be handled very carefully.

See also **radioactivity; nuclear power; nuclear weapon; cosmic ray;** and **X ray.**

radio

In the 1800s, the telegraph sent messages over hundreds of miles almost instantly. But telegraph messages must travel through wires. In 1895, the Italian inventor Guglielmo Marconi found a way to send radio signals through the air without wires. Since radio waves may be sent anywhere—even through walls—people everywhere can receive the signals. Airplane pilots flying over the earth and astronauts traveling through space use radio to talk with people on the ground. You know from experience that no matter where you are, your radio can pick up a variety of programs. In England, people still call radio the *wireless.*

Early radios were large and needed lots of electricity. Today, battery-powered radios can be carried anywhere.

Radio signals are invisible electrical waves that are sent from a transmitter to a receiver—a radio. When you listen to the radio, you are hearing sound that was changed to electrical signals and then changed back to sound.

A microphone changes sound to an electrical signal. The signal is not powerful enough to travel far, so it is passed through a *transmitter*. The transmitter strengthens the signal and mixes it with powerful electromagnetic waves, called *carrier waves*. Then the signal is broadcast from a *sending antenna*. The signal travels out in all directions at the speed of light—300,000 kilometers (186,000 miles) per second.

The antenna of your radio catches several radio signals at once. The *tuner* lets you select the signal of a particular *frequency*. Then the radio's *amplifier* strengthens the signal and sends it to the *speakers*. The speakers vibrate to produce sound. Even tiny radios can make sound loud and clear.

Like all electromagnetic waves, a radio signal travels in waves. The frequency is the number of times per second the wave moves up and down. Signals on the AM band of a radio are measured in *kilohertz*—thousands of cycles per second. If a station broadcasts at 880 kilohertz, its signals have a frequency of 880,000 cycles per second. Signals on the FM band of a radio are measured in *megahertz*—millions of cycles per second.

Two-way radios have their own special frequencies. If you have used a walkie-talkie, you have used a two-way radio. Pilots use two-way radio to talk with air controllers. Ships, police cars, buses, and taxis are equipped with two-way radio. Many people use citizens band radio—CB—to listen and talk to others.

radioactivity

Some elements are radioactive. When their atoms *decay*—break down—they send out small particles from the nucleus—the atom's center. Sometimes, the loss of these particles turns the atom into the atom of a different element. Uranium, radium, and plutonium are elements that naturally have a high level of radioactivity. Many elements can be made radioactive.

Only some of the atoms of a radioactive material decay at a time. The amount of time it takes for half of the atoms in a radioactive material to decay is called that element's *half-life*. After half of the atoms have decayed, then it takes another half-life for half of the remaining atoms to decay. The half-life of some radioactive elements is only a matter of seconds. For others, such as uranium, the half-life is millions of years.

A radio station turns sound into radio signals (top). A receiver turns the signals back into sound (bottom).

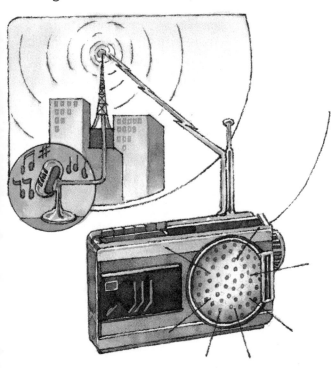

Important Radioactive Elements

uranium-235 and uranium-238 are fuels for nuclear reactors and weapons.

radium is used as a radioactive source for x-ray and medical radiation devices.

carbon-14 and potassium-40 are used in dating of ancient artifacts and rocks.

hydrogen-3, also called *tritium*, is a possible fuel for nuclear fusion.

radio telescope

Three types of energy are released by radiation—alpha particles, beta particles, and gamma rays. Alpha particles consist of two protons and two neutrons. Beta particles are electrons. Gamma rays are high-energy X rays. (*See* **radiation; electron;** and **X ray.**)

Radioactivity cannot be seen or felt, but its effects can be long-lasting and sometimes harmful. Small amounts are used by doctors to treat some illnesses. But radioactivity can destroy living tissue and change the genes in cells. Large amounts can make a person very sick and cause cancer. People who work with radioactive materials must wear protective clothing. Radioactive materials must be carefully stored.

In 1896, a French scientist named Henri Becquerel discovered radioactivity. He was studying minerals that glow in the dark after exposure to sunlight. He recorded their glow on photographic paper. One day when it was too cloudy to experiment, he kept the minerals and paper in a drawer. Later, when he looked at the paper, he was surprised to see that even though the paper was still in its wrapper, it had become foggy. The minerals contained uranium. Becquerel decided that the uranium was giving off energy that went through the wrapping and was recorded on the paper. (*See* **uranium.**)

Several years later, Marie and Pierre Curie became interested in Becquerel's mysterious rays. The Curies discovered that most of the radiation from uranium actually comes from two other elements found in tiny amounts in uranium ore. These elements are radium and polonium. (*See* **Curie, Marie and Pierre.**)

radio telescope

Many objects in outer space give off radio waves, including our sun, the planet Jupiter, and even whole galaxies. Astronomers who want to study these sources of radio waves can use a radio telescope.

In some ways, a radio telescope is similar to an ordinary radio. In both a radio and a radio telescope, an antenna collects radio

The antenna of a huge radio telescope in New Mexico. The signals received can be translated into pictures (above).

waves. In a radio, electronic circuits change these waves into sounds you can hear. A radio telescope, too, has an antenna and electronic equipment to receive incoming radio waves. But the antenna of a radio telescope is much bigger and more complicated—often it is a large dish-shaped structure. Big antennas are needed to collect weak radio signals coming from far off in space.

Radio telescopes differ from ordinary radios in another important way. The telescope's electronic equipment does not change radio waves into sound. Instead, it changes them into pictures. The pictures show dark areas for strong sources of radio waves, and light areas for weak or background sources. That makes it possible for astronomers to locate and study sources of radio waves that are far away, even in other galaxies.

See also **radio** and **astronomy.**

radium

Radium is a white metallic element that is *radioactive*. This means that tiny invisible particles and X rays continuously shoot out from it. If too many of these particles and rays enter our bodies, they can kill us or cause cancer and other serious illnesses. Radium also gives off continuous heat and light. (*See* **radioactivity**.)

Small amounts of radium have been used in medicine to destroy cancers. Radium mixed with phosphorus compounds causes them to glow brightly. These glowing compounds used to be put on watch dials to make them visible in the dark. But radium is very dangerous, and the people who painted the watch dials often developed cancer. Today, cheaper and safer substances are used instead.

Since its discovery in 1898 by Marie and Pierre Curie, about 4.5 kilograms (10 pounds) of radium have been found. Radium is so radioactive—it shoots out so many of its particles—that one-tenth of any given amount disappears every 250 years. There would not be any radium in the world if two other elements, uranium and thorium, did not form radium when they break down. The radium that disappears becomes a radioactive gas called *radon*.

See also **Curie, Marie and Pierre.**

railroad

Railroads are major means of transportation in many countries. The building of railroads has played an important role in the development of large areas of Canada and the United States. People were eager to settle in areas reached by good transportation. Farmers and ranchers could ship their products by rail to faraway cities and ports.

The first railroads were very different from railroads of today. In the 1600s and early 1700s, horses pulled wagons with wooden wheels along wooden rails. These early trains carried only coal and ore.

Steel rails replaced wooden ones in the middle 1700s, and inventors began to experiment with steam engines. In 1801, Richard Trevithick, an Englishman, built a steam locomotive that could pull a heavy load at nearly 32 kilometers (20 miles) per hour.

In 1828, the Baltimore and Ohio Railroad became the first railroad in the United States to carry passengers. Other passenger lines soon spread across the Eastern United States. New York, Boston, Baltimore, and other East Coast cities became major railroad centers. Towns grew up along the rail lines. On May 10, 1869, the Union Pacific and Central Pacific railroads came together at Promontory, Utah. Together, they formed the first rail line that ran from the Atlantic to the Pacific coast.

During the rest of the 1800s, thousands of miles of track were laid. By 1900, every state and territory in the United States had at least one railway line. Today, the United States alone has more than 640,000 kilometers (400,000 miles) of railways—enough to reach all the way to the moon and two-thirds of the way back!

Railroad Track It takes about 176 sections of rail to build 1.6 kilometers (1 mile) of railway track. Each section is about 10 meters (30 feet) long. Before the rails are set in place, a *bed* must be prepared. The bed is the foundation on which the track is laid.

Preparing the bed begins with *grading* —smoothing the ground. Next, gravel or

An engineer's drawing of an early French locomotive.

An Amtrak train crosses a high trestle, giving passengers a spectacular view.

crushed rock is spread on the bed to allow water to drain from under the rails. Heavy wooden beams, called *ties,* are then set across the bed about 50 centimeters (20 inches) apart. Each tie is about 2.5 meters (8 feet) long. The rails are laid on top of the ties and hammered into place with heavy steel spikes. Teams of workers laid the track by hand until a track-laying machine was invented in 1905.

Unlike cars and trucks, trains cannot make sharp turns, so tracks are laid as straight as possible. If the track has to curve, the curve is long and gradual. Tracks must also be as level as possible. Instead of going straight up and down a mountain, the track goes back and forth to the top in gradual curves. Often, tunnels are blasted through steep mountains. Strong bridges are built for track that must cross rivers, lakes, and gorges.

The two rails on which a train travels must be *parallel*—the same distance apart at all points. This distance is called the *gauge.* In the early days, different railroads often used their own gauges. This meant that trains of one line could not travel on tracks of another line. In the 1880s, the

FREIGHT TRAIN

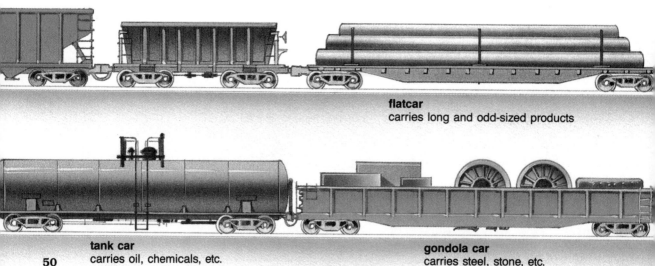

flatcar
carries long and odd-sized products

tank car
carries oil, chemicals, etc.

gondola car
carries steel, stone, etc.

A Japanese bullet train speeds through the countryside at more than 200 miles per hour.

United States government set the gauge for all rail lines in the country to 1.4 meters (4 feet 8½ inches).

Two-Way Train Traffic A railroad track is like a one-way street. All trains must travel on it in one direction. Many railway lines have double sets of tracks for two-way traffic. Two-way traffic is also possible if the track has *sidings*—short lines of track that extend off the main line. One train gets out of the way of an oncoming train by going onto the siding. After the oncoming train has passed, the train waiting on the siding can move ahead to the main track again.

The train crew can start a train, stop it, control its speed, and back it up. But they do not steer the train. Its direction is controlled by the rails. When a train must leave one line of track to travel on another, a *switch* moves part of the track over to meet the rails going in the new direction. Switches are short rails that can be moved because of the way they are mounted. They are used to get a train off the main line onto a siding and then back. Switches move trains from express to local tracks, and from west-bound lines to north-bound lines. When tracks cross each other, switches let one train

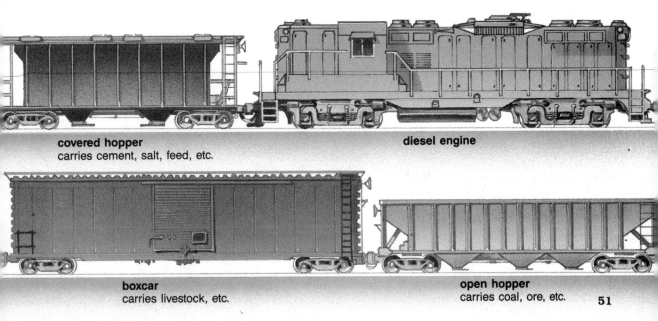

covered hopper
carries cement, salt, feed, etc.

diesel engine

boxcar
carries livestock, etc.

open hopper
carries coal, ore, etc.

through first, then the other. Switches used to be operated by hand. Today, almost all track switches are run by machines.

To operate a train safely, a train engineer needs information about the track ahead. Have switches been properly set? Is another train stopped ahead? Is the bridge out? Lights and other signals along the track give a train crew much of the information it needs. Additional information is supplied by two-way radio contact between train crews and control stations. Busy stations use computers to keep track of traffic, switches, and signals.

Railroad Workers More than 1 million people work to keep railroads running in the United States. Many work on the trains as engineers, crew members, ticket takers, and baggage and freight-handlers. Others operate stations, switching and signal systems, and communications. Although few new rail lines are being laid today, people are needed to inspect, maintain, and repair all the miles of track in use. Inspectors and maintenance crews must constantly work to make sure that track beds, rails, bridges, switches, and signals are in good working order.

Like all machines, trains must be maintained. Locomotives and cars are inspected and kept in repair by crews in train yards.

Kinds of Trains A train is made up of a *locomotive*—engine—and the cars it pulls. The locomotives of 100 years ago were powered by steam. Diesel-electric locomotives were introduced in 1924. By the 1950s, diesel-electric had replaced most steam engines. A modern locomotive can travel nearly 160 kilometers (100 miles) per hour. Some newer trains can travel twice as fast.

A locomotive pulls passenger cars or freight cars or both. Commuter cars, also called *coach cars*, carry passengers short distances. Passengers who travel longer distances use trains with sleeper cars, dining cars, and baggage cars.

There are many kinds of freight cars. Various tank cars carry liquids and compressed gases. Refrigerator cars are used to carry

foods that must be kept cold. Flatbed cars can carry anything—bulky tanks, lumber, or new automobiles.

Today, freight is often *containerized*—put in large containers. The containers are driven by truck to railroad freight yards and loaded onto flatbed cars. They travel by rail to another freight yard, and are then loaded onto other trucks for final delivery.

Piggybacking is similar to containerizing freight. Loaded trucks are driven onto flatbed cars and carried by train to an unloading area near to the trucks' final destination. Some passenger trains have piggybacking for carrying passengers' automobiles.

Trucks and aircraft have taken over much of the work that railroads used to do. But even today, millions of people and billions of tons of goods travel each year by rail.

See also **subway.**

rain

Rain is drops of water that fall from clouds. Most of the water that falls as rain comes from oceans, lakes, and rivers. Their water is constantly *evaporating*—changing from a liquid to an invisible gas. This gas, called *water vapor,* goes into the air. Plants, animals, and volcanoes release water vapor into the air, too.

A rain gauge is a container with a scale. It measures how much rain has fallen.

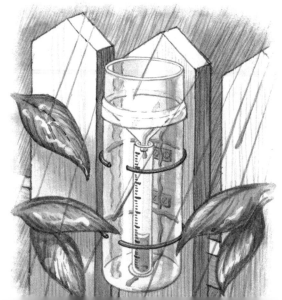

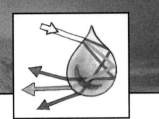

A rainbow occurs when drops of water break sunlight into light of different colors (right).

Water vapor has less mass than air, so it drifts upward. At the higher, cooler levels of the atmosphere, the water vapor cools to its *dew point*. At this temperature, it changes to a liquid and forms tiny water drops around specks of dust.

As billions of water drops form in an area, they become a cloud. When the temperature of a cloud is above freezing, the tiny water drops bump into each other and combine, making larger water drops. In most cases, the cloud passes through a freezing area and the drops turn into ice. If the ice particles are large, they may be too heavy to stay up. They start to fall as snowflakes. When the snowflakes pass through warmer air, they melt and fall to the ground as raindrops. If the drops are tiny, the rain is called *drizzle*. Drizzle may take an hour or more to reach the ground. If falling raindrops pass through a layer of freezing air, they may turn to *sleet*. If the air is cold enough all the way down, the snowflakes do not melt.

Some factories pollute the air with gases. The gases combine with the water in the atmosphere, making it slightly acid. The water falls as *acid rain*. It pollutes lakes, streams, and soil. Few plants and animals can survive in areas polluted by acid rain.

Meteorologists—scientists who study the weather—use an instrument called a *rain gauge* to measure the amount of rain that falls during a certain period of time. Light rain falls at less than 0.5 millimeters per hour (1/50 inches per hour). Heavy rain falls at more than 4 millimeters per hour (8/50 inches per hour).

The heaviest rain usually occurs during a hurricane or thunderstorm, and may cause flooding. An island in the Indian Ocean holds the record for receiving the most rainfall in 24 hours. On March 15 to 16, 1952, nearly 1,880 millimeters (74 inches) of rain fell. Cherrapunji, India, holds the record for receiving the most rainfall in a 12-month period. In 1860 to 1861, over 26,420 millimeters (1,057 inches) of rain pounded the region.

See also **atmosphere; cloud; dew; flood; hurricane; snow;** and **thunderstorm.**

rainbow

A rainbow is a giant arch of colored bands that may curve across the sky just after a rain. Rainbows appear when the sun shines through raindrops still in the air.

Although sunlight looks clear, it is actually a mixture of seven colors. When sunlight strikes a raindrop, the rays of each color bend a certain amount. The sunlight separates into a band of colors called the *spectrum*. The inner surface of the raindrop reflects the light and sends it back in the direction from which it came. The rays are bent again as they leave the raindrop. A rainbow results when many raindrops in the air bend and reflect the rays of sunlight.

Red forms the outer edge of the rainbow, followed by orange, yellow, green, blue, and indigo, with violet on the inside. You can remember the order of colors by using the first letter of each color to spell the name of an imaginary boy—ROY G. BIV.

To see a rainbow, you must stand with your back to the sun. Sometimes you may see a second, fainter, rainbow outside the first. The second rainbow occurs when sunlight is reflected twice before it leaves the raindrops. The order of the colors is reversed, with red on the inside and violet on the outside.

See also **color** and **light.**

rain forest

Rain forests grow in areas that receive more than 203 centimeters (80 inches) of rainfall each year. Most of these areas are around the equator in South America, Africa, and Asia. These rain forests are also warm. Temperatures are between 21° C (70° F) and 34° C (95° F) all year. There are a few cool rain forests. One of these is on the Olympic Peninsula of Washington State.

Plants of the Rain Forest   A rain forest is sometimes called a *jungle,* but it is not. A jungle is so dense with vines and plants that it is hard to travel through it. But in a rain forest, the trees grow very tall. Their tops form a high *canopy* that shades the forest

floor. Very few plants can grow in this shade, so it is easy to walk through.

The tall trees in a rain forest act as supports for other plants to grow on. Many kinds of vines grow around the trees and up to the light. Most of them do not harm the trees on which they grow. The *strangler vine* is an exception. As it grows, it slowly wraps around the tree and chokes off the tree's light, water, and food.

Trees in a rain forest give flowers a place to grow. Orchids, some kinds of ferns and mosses, and other *epiphytes* grow on the upper surfaces of branches. Epiphytes are sometimes called *air plants.* They get their food and moisture from the air. They do not need soil for their roots. Their perch on a tree branch puts them closer to the sunlight they need to make their own food. When these plants bloom, they form a colorful garden high above the forest floor.

In most forests, there are only a few kinds of trees, with many of each kind. But in a rain forest, 60 to 100 different kinds of trees may grow on a single acre of land. You may have to go quite a distance before you find two trees of the same kind.

Rain forests are moist and warm (left), providing good living conditions for many living things. The channel-billed toucan (right) lives in South American rain forests.

Animals of the Rain Forest   The rain forest has a larger variety of living things than any other biome. Besides many kinds of plants, there is a wide variety of animals. More than half of them are insects. Ants, termites, flies, bees, and butterflies are especially plentiful. (*See* **biome.**)

Many snakes live in rain forests, including the world's largest snake—the anaconda. Some of the snakes of the rain forests, such as the cobra and bushmaster, are poisonous. But most snakes in the rain forests are shy and stay hidden. They do not attack people unless they are threatened.

Frogs are common rain-forest residents. In drier biomes, frogs must live near water. In the rain forest, the air is so moist that frogs are found almost everywhere. Many live in trees. The suction cups on their feet hold them on the trunks and branches. Some lay their eggs in water, but others carry their eggs on their backs. Tadpoles grow into tiny frogs inside the eggs on their parents' backs.

The capybara—the largest rodent in the world—lives in the South American rain forest. The capybara looks like a giant guinea pig and weighs about 54 kilograms (120 pounds). It lives along rivers and feeds on plants. Deer, too, are found here, but they are small compared to the deer of North America. The mouse deer is only 30 centimeters (1 foot) tall.

Monkeys and apes are among the noisier residents of a tropical rain forest. Most monkeys and some apes spend most of their lives high in the treetops. Monkeys of Asia and Africa swing through the trees, hand-over-hand. Monkeys of South America use their long tails as well as their hands to help them travel. Chimpanzees and gorillas live in tropical rain forests, too, but they spend most of their time on the forest floor.

Birds are a colorful part of the tropical rain forest. This is the place to see parrots, toucans, macaws, hummingbirds, pigeons, harpy eagles, hawks, and owls. Many of the brightly colored birds in pet stores come from the rain forests.

People and Rain Forests   Humans are affecting rain forests in an important way. A few tribes living in the rain forests are still hunters and gatherers, and live in the rain forests without disturbing them. But many people want to turn this land into farms to grow crops for food. To do this, they cut down trees and vines and burn them. Then they plant their crops. But after a year or two, crops do not grow well, so more forest is cut and burned.

The problem with growing crops in rain forests is that the soil is thin and not very rich. Many leaves fall to the ground and decay rapidly. The decayed leaves make good fertilizer for plants, but the constant rain quickly washes these substances away. When a rain forest is cut for farming, the first crop uses up all the substances. Large parts of the world's rain forests have been destroyed by this kind of farming.

Raleigh, Sir Walter

Sir Walter Raleigh was an English soldier, adventurer, and writer. His interest in exploration led to the founding of the first English colony in North America.

Raleigh was born in 1554. According to legend, he once spread his cloak over a puddle so Queen Elizabeth I could walk over it without getting her feet muddy. The queen liked Raleigh and gave him land in Ireland and the right to start colonies in America.

In 1585, Raleigh sent a small group of men to America. They set up a colony on Roanoke Island, off the coast of North Carolina, but it failed. In 1597, Raleigh sent more than 100 new colonists to Roanoke Island. But when a ship came from England with supplies three years later, the whole colony had disappeared without a trace.

Queen Elizabeth became angry with Raleigh when she found out he planned to marry one of her maids of honor. After Elizabeth died, King James I accused Raleigh of treason and imprisoned him in the Tower of London. There Raleigh lived comfortably for

13 years, with his wife, son, and servants. In prison, he wrote a book about world history. King James released Raleigh in 1616 and ordered him to find gold in South America, but steer clear of Spanish settlements. Raleigh attacked Spanish settlements anyway. When he returned to England in 1618—without having found the gold—King James had him put to death.

ranch

A ranch is a large farm where animals such as sheep, horses, or beef cattle are raised. Smaller animals, such as mink, may be raised on ranches, too. *Dude ranches* are resorts where tourists can get a taste of life in the Old West.

The average ranch in the American West covers more than 3,000 acres (1,200 hectares). Cattle and sheep ranches are large, because each animal needs several acres of grassland for grazing. In Australia and New Zealand, a ranch is called a *station*. A station may cover millions of square miles.

Below, cattle roam free, seeking food. At right, cowboys *brand* a cow— mark it with the ranch's symbol.

In the 1800s, American ranchers raised their cattle on government land. This land was called *open range* because it was not divided by fences. Cattle belonging to many ranches grazed together. A few months after a calf was born, it was branded with the symbol of the ranch that owned it. Once a year, cowboys rounded up the cattle from each ranch and drove them across the prairie to markets. (*See* cowboy.)

Today, even though cattle graze in large fenced areas, they are still branded. Ranchers tend to the fences and herd the animals by jeep or even helicopter. Besides preparing sheep for market, sheep ranchers also shear the animals for their wool.

See also farming.

Raphael

The artist known as Raphael was one of the most important painters and designers of the Renaissance period. The Renaissance was a time of great developments in the arts and sciences. It started in Europe during the 1300s. (*See* **Renaissance.**)

Raphael was born Raffaello Sanzio in 1483 in Urbino, Italy. His father, who was an artist, sent his son to study with Perugino, a famous Italian painter. Perugino taught Raphael about the newest styles of Italian art.

Raphael moved to Florence, Italy, in 1504. There, he studied works by the important artists Leonardo da Vinci and Michelangelo. Both men painted people and scenes in a realistic way. Raphael was greatly influenced by their styles. (*See* **Leonardo da Vinci** and **Michelangelo.**)

Raphael's paintings of Jesus and his mother, Mary, were unlike those of most other artists of his time. They showed the mother and child as graceful, natural figures. Though it was clear that they were holy people, Raphael made them look very human.

The paintings of Mary and Jesus caught the eye of Pope Julius II, the leader of the Roman Catholic Church. In 1508, Julius invited Raphael to Rome. Raphael spent three years creating *frescoes*—paintings on damp plaster—for the walls of the pope's palace. The frescoes showed scenes of religious figures with common people. No one before Raphael had ever created paintings that made religious events seem so natural and human.

Raphael lived for nine more years after finishing the frescoes in 1511. During that time, he planned and carried out a great many works of art. He trained students and assistants who helped to create the works.

Raphael completed additional frescoes and paintings for Pope Julius and his successor, Pope Leo X. He drew portraits of famous Romans and designed wall hangings and sculptures. He also began creating designs for buildings. At the time of his death,

This painting by Raphael shows Mary as the *Madonna*—the mother of Jesus.

Raphael was directing the building of St. Peter's Church in Rome.

Raphael died in 1520, after a short illness. He was only 37 years old. Many of his paintings were copied onto *engravings*—designs scratched into metal—so that they could be printed over and over. This way, many artists saw pictures of his works and were influenced by his style.

See also **architecture; sculpture;** and **painters and painting.**

rat

Rats are *rodents*—furry mammals with sharp front teeth designed for gnawing. They are bigger than mice and have longer tails. Rats generally weigh 0.5 kilogram (1 pound) or less. They are strong and nimble. They can climb walls, swim across rivers, and wiggle through small holes.

There are more than 100 kinds of rats. Most live in warm, tropical lands. The Norway rat and the black rat are found in just about every part of the world. These rats eat almost anything and live almost anywhere—in open country and in cities. They

reading

Scientists use white rats in experiments. The black rat is a serious pest.

reproduce very rapidly. A pair of black or Norway rats may live only a year. But at the end of that time, they may have produced almost 100 offspring and thousands of descendents!

Rats—especially black and Norway rats—eat or destroy up to one-fifth of the world's food crops each year. They carry many diseases, including typhus, rabies, and bubonic plague. (*See* **plague.**)

On the other hand, rats are useful research animals. Albino Norway rats raised in laboratories have helped scientists learn about health and find cures for many human illnesses.

See also **rodent.**

reading

Reading is the skill of understanding printed or written words and sentences. It is one of the most basic and important skills a person can have. It is also one of the most enjoyable, making it possible for you to know the world's great stories and poems. By reading aloud to friends, you can share what you have liked reading.

Most people read thousands of words each day without ever opening a book. We read signs everywhere. We read letters from friends and the labels on packages and bottles. We read the words that appear at the start of movies and television shows.

People read books, newspapers, and magazines for information, pleasure, or both. Reading introduces a person to new or different ideas. A "how-to" book can teach you a hobby or how to build something. Students read textbooks to learn about subjects taught in school. When they study, they read the notes they took in class. Reading also helps people relax during their free time. Adventure stories, love stories, and detective stories provide hours of enjoyment.

Most people learn to read when they are children. Children begin to recognize words by their shapes. These are usually the words they see on signs and labels, and in simple books. Next, children begin to understand groups of words that make short sentences. With practice, the child comes to understand the ideas presented in longer sentences.

As people read more, they add new words to their *vocabularies.* A person's vocabulary is the collection of words he or she can use properly when writing or speaking. When readers come across a word they do not recognize, they turn to a *dictionary* for

Building Your Vocabulary

Your *vocabulary* is the group of words you recognize, understand, and use. Increasing your vocabulary can make reading easier.

If you come across a word you do not know, follow these steps:

1. Guess what the word means from the way it is used in the sentence. Is it a name of something (a noun)? Is it an action word (a verb)? Is it a modifier (an adjective or adverb)?

2. Look up the word in a dictionary. The definition will tell you what the word means. The dictionary will also help you to pronounce and spell the word.

3. Write down the word and its meaning in a notebook. Use the word in a sentence.

4. Ask a parent or teacher for help in understanding hard words.

help. A dictionary is a book that lists words and their meanings. Sometimes, how the word is used in a sentence provides a clue to its meaning. For example, if you read, "The okapi is related to the camel," you can probably figure out that an okapi is an animal. You can use a dictionary to learn more about the word's meaning and *pronunciation*—the correct way to say it. (*See* **dictionary.**)

Millions of people around the world are *illiterate*—unable to read or write. But people can learn to read at any age. Governments are trying to wipe out illiteracy.

See also **learning.**

Reagan, Ronald

Ronald Reagan was the 40th president of the United States. He served for two terms. When Reagan was elected for his first term as president in 1980, he was 69 years old—the oldest man ever elected president. When he was reelected in 1984, he won by a huge margin.

Reagan was born in 1911 in Tampico, Illinois. He graduated from Eureka College in 1932. One of his first jobs was as a radio sports announcer. In 1937, he was hired as an actor by Warner Brothers Studio in California. Over the next 25 years, Reagan appeared in many movies and on television. He served in the army during World War II. In 1947, he was elected president of the Screen Actors Guild, a group that represents movie actors and actresses.

In 1962, Reagan joined the Republican Party and became active in politics. In 1964, he made a speech on television for Barry M. Goldwater, the Republican candidate for president. Reagan criticized high taxes and said that the U.S. government spent too much money on some of its programs.

Reagan's experience as an actor made him a convincing speaker. His speech gained him the support of many people who shared his views. In 1966, he was elected governor of California. He was reelected in 1970 and served as governor until 1975.

Ronald Reagan was elected to a second term as president in 1984.

Only about two months after Reagan took office as president in 1981, a gunman tried to kill him. The man, John Hinckley, was later judged to be insane. President Reagan stayed in the hospital for many weeks, but recovered fully from his wounds.

As president, Reagan worked to reduce taxes and to cut the amount of money spent by the government. Critics said his plans helped the rich and hurt the poor. Reagan also tried to increase the military power of the United States. He appointed Sandra Day O'Connor to the Supreme Court—the first woman Supreme Court judge. During his second term, Reagan outlined a plan that would make the federal tax system simpler and fairer. Congress worked on this plan and passed it into law.

Reagan was very popular for most of his presidency. But in 1986, the way he ran the executive branch of the government came under harsh criticism. Late that year, it was discovered that some of his advisers had done something against the law. They had sent money to a group of soldiers fighting against the government of Nicaragua, a Central American country. Reagan said he had been unaware of this, but would take responsibility for their actions.

A real estate agent helps people buy, sell, or rent land and buildings.

real estate

The total of everything that someone owns is called that person's *estate*. A person's estate may consist of two kinds of property —personal property and real estate. Personal property is anything that can be moved around easily. Cars and television sets are personal property. Real estate—also called *real property*—is property that cannot be moved easily. Land and everything attached to it are considered real estate. This includes trees, houses, bridges, and other structures—and even minerals buried in the earth.

Real estate can be bought and sold by businesses and by individual people. Ownership of real estate is passed from one person to another by a *deed.* A deed is a legal document that names the owner of the property. When real estate is sold or given to another, the deed is signed by the original owner and given to the new owner.

Many people do not own their houses or apartments, and many businesses do not own their factories or offices. Instead, they *rent* from the owner—pay the owner a fee for use of the property.

In much of Europe during the Middle Ages, land was not bought and sold as it is today. It was owned by the king. If someone did something for the king, such as fighting in a war, the king might give that person a piece of land to rule and care for. This person made sure that the fields produced crops and that the forests were protected. But the king remained the owner of the land.

In England at that time, property owned by a person was called a *freehold estate.* There were several kinds of freehold estates. One kind was the *life estate.* A life estate was property owned by a person as long as he lived. When he died, the original owner of the property got it back. A *fee-tail estate* was property that the owner could pass on to his *heirs*—children or other people who receive a person's property after his or her death. A *fee-simple estate* was property with which the owner could do anything he wanted.

Most estates were life estates or fee-tail estates. If the owner died without any heirs, such property went back to the king. Today, almost all real estate is fee-simple. The owner can decide whether to keep it, give it away, sell it, or pass it on to heirs.

recording, *see* sound recording; video recording

Red Sea

The Red Sea is a body of water that lies between Africa and the Middle East. To the south and west are the countries of Egypt, the Sudan, and Ethiopia. To the north is the Arabian Peninsula.

In the late 1800s, the Red Sea became a busy waterway. The Suez Canal, opened in 1869, connected the northern end of the Red Sea to the Mediterranean Sea. This made it possible for ships to travel from Europe and North Africa through the canal and the Red Sea and into the Indian Ocean. Before the canal, ships had to sail thousands of miles around the southern tip of Africa.

The Red Sea is about 1,400 miles (2,240 kilometers) long and covers an area larger

Both redwoods and giant sequoias can live a long time. Some of the redwoods are more than 2,000 years old. Some of the giant sequoias are even older. They are thought to be more than 3,000 years old.

The people at the foot of this sequoia help show how large it really is.

than the state of California. It is surrounded by dry, barren country. There are no large cities on its shores. Its name probably comes from the reddish algae or seaweed that grows in its waters.

The waters of the Red Sea are warm and very salty. The surface temperature of the water is about 85° F (29° C). The weather is so warm that water evaporates quickly from the Red Sea, leaving its salt behind.

redwoods and sequoias

The sequoia is a kind of evergreen tree that grows along the northern California coast. The *redwood* and the *giant sequoia* belong to this group of trees. Both grow in thin, rocky soil in areas too dry for other trees.

Redwoods grow on hillsides along the coast and get moisture from the coastal fog. They have small, green, needlelike leaves. Redwoods may be the tallest trees in the world. One tree is 110 meters (368 feet) tall and 13.2 meters (44 feet) around.

Giant sequoias grow on the western slopes of the Sierra Nevada—a mountain range in California. They have scalelike, bluish leaves. These trees sometimes grow to more than 100 meters (300 feet). One giant sequoia, named General Sherman, measures 30.3 meters (101½ feet) around its trunk. Cars can drive through a tunnel in its base.

A third kind of sequoia, the *dawn redwood,* was thought to be extinct. Then, in 1943, it was rediscovered in China.

Reed, Walter

Walter Reed was a United States Army doctor. He proved that yellow fever is spread by mosquitoes. Yellow fever is a very serious disease that often causes death. Before the 1900s, outbreaks of yellow fever occurred frequently in the seaports of South America, Central America, and the United States. People knew that yellow fever could spread rapidly, but they did not know how it spread.

Reed was sent to Cuba to study yellow fever among U.S. troops stationed there. He carried out experiments to find out how the disease spread. He exposed one group of men to the clothes and bedding used by yellow-fever victims. These men did not get the disease. Other men bitten by mosquitoes did develop yellow fever. The cause of the disease proved to be a *virus.* Viruses are microscopic structures responsible for many diseases. A mosquito can pick up the virus by biting someone who has yellow fever. When the mosquito bites another person, it passes on the virus. (*See* **mosquitoes and gnats** and **virus.**)

After Reed's experiments, efforts were made to clean up mosquito-breeding sites in Cuba. Yellow fever all but vanished in Cuba. Mosquito-breeding sites were also cleaned up in Panama. This made it possible to build the Panama Canal.

reef

A reef is a place in the ocean where sand, rock, or coral has built up, making the water shallow. Some tall reefs break the surface of the water. Reefs provide homes for fish and other sea life, but reefs can be dangerous for ships.

Most of the world's reefs are made of the skeletons of coral animals. These skeletons are hard limestone. Living corals attach themselves to the skeletons of dead corals. As layer upon layer of coral builds up, the reefs grow in height and width. Since most corals live in warm, shallow water, most coral reefs are found in the warm South Pacific Ocean. (*See* **coral.**)

An *atoll* is one kind of coral reef. It is a small, low island shaped like a ring or horseshoe. A shallow body of water known as a *lagoon* is in its center. An atoll is formed by coral growing around the sides of an underground mountain or volcano.

A coral reef is made of the skeletons of millions of tiny coral animals. Many small sea creatures live in coral reefs.

A *barrier reef* is another kind of coral reef. It forms in shallow water near the shore of an island or continent. The Great Barrier Reef along eastern Australia is the world's longest barrier reef. It stretches over 2,000 kilometers (1,200 miles).

See also **island.**

Reformation

The Reformation was a religious movement that began in Europe in the early 1500s. Many of the Christian churches we know today grew out of the ideas and beliefs of the Reformation.

In 1500, nearly all the people who lived in Europe belonged to a single Christian church. The church was headed by the pope. The popes had become very powerful political leaders. Even kings obeyed them. The popes not only led the church, but they ruled many people and owned huge estates. For centuries, popes and other church leaders had used church money to build both costly churches and rich palaces for themselves. They told the people that God would bless those who gave money to the church. They thought spiritual power and political power went together.

Many people began to think that the church had become too worldly. They thought the church should pay more attention to people's spiritual needs, and less to wealth and power. They wanted to *reform* the church—change and improve it. The movement they began was called the Reformation. The people who supported the Reformation were called Protestants because they were protesting against some practices of the church.

One of the first reformers was a German monk and teacher named Martin Luther. In 1517, he made a list of his disagreements with church leaders. He hung the list on the door of the church in the town where he lived. Luther said that people could not buy or earn God's blessing. He said they needed faith first of all.

John Calvin began a new church in Switzerland in the 1500s.

The pope and other church leaders ordered Luther to stop teaching and writing, but he would not. Luther and his followers started a new church. The churches that followed Luther's teachings were called Lutheran. (*See* **Luther, Martin.**)

Another early reformer was John Calvin. He lived and preached in Switzerland. Calvin said that Christians should follow the Bible, not what was told to them by church leaders. His ideas spread to the Netherlands and Scotland, and later to England. In the Netherlands, Calvin's followers began the Reformed church. In Scotland, his followers began the Presbyterian church. Many of the English settlers who came to North America in the 1600s were followers of Calvin. They were called Puritans.

The old church came to be known as the Roman Catholic Church. In the middle 1500s, its leaders made many changes to help their church make a new beginning. The Roman Catholic church remained very powerful. Today, most people in southern Europe and Ireland are Roman Catholics. Most people in Britain and northern Europe are members of churches that began in the Reformation.

See also **Protestant churches; Roman Catholic Church;** and **Christianity.**

refrigeration

Try this experiment. Dip your hand in warm water, then blow on it. Even though the water is warm and your breath is warm, your hand feels cool as the water *evaporates* —turns from a liquid to a gas. Evaporation removes heat from your skin.

Refrigeration, too, cools by evaporation. It requires special liquids, called *refrigerants,* that evaporate at low temperatures. In your refrigerator, the refrigerant moves through cooling coils to remove the heat from inside.

The *evaporator* suddenly reduces pressure on the liquid refrigerant, causing it to evaporate. As it evaporates, the refrigerant travels through coils in the walls of the freezer. It absorbs heat, making the freezer very cold. Then the refrigerant enters the *condenser,* which turns it back into a liquid. Now it is very warm. It travels through condensing coils outside the refrigerator, giving up some of its heat to the outside air.

Cooling fluid removes heat from the refrigerator's freezer (top).

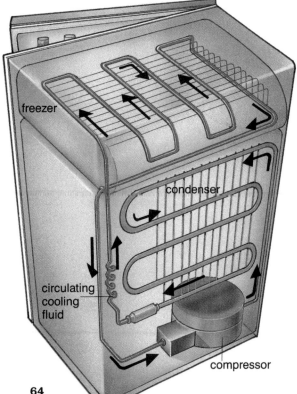

freezer

condenser

circulating cooling fluid

compressor

The same refrigerant is pumped over and over through the cooling coils. The faster the refrigerant circulates through the coils, the colder the temperature becomes inside the refrigerator. The temperature in a refrigerator is kept steady by a *thermostat.* A thermostat is a switch that can be set to turn on and off at certain temperatures. When the temperature gets too cold, the thermostat turns off the compressor. When the temperature gets too warm, the thermostat turns on the compressor.

One of the first refrigerating machines was built in 1834 by Jacob Perkins, a U.S. engineer. His machine was big, and was used in large meat-packing and ice-making plants. In 1913, A. H. Goss, another American, built a smaller refrigerator for home use. Before then, people kept food cold in *iceboxes.* These were thick wooden chests with a compartment to hold blocks of ice. Iceboxes needed daily deliveries of ice.

Refrigeration has other uses besides preserving foods. It is used to change the elements oxygen, nitrogen, and hydrogen from gases into *super-cold* liquids. A super-cold liquid does not freeze. Liquid oxygen and other liquefied gases are used in medicine and industry. Liquid oxygen is a main ingredient in rocket fuel.

Another use of refrigeration is in cooling rooms and buildings. (*See* **air conditioning.**)

religion

A religion is a set of beliefs and practices that people use to worship a power greater than themselves. For millions of people, this power is God. Others believe that different gods or forces influence their lives.

There are many reasons why people practice a religion. Religion helps people feel that their lives have meaning and purpose. Through prayer, they ask God to guide and protect them. Religion helps them to understand the difference between what is right and what is wrong. Most religions also teach that there is a life after death.

MAJOR WORLD RELIGIONS

About half of the people in the world follow one of these major religions.

Religion	Number of followers
Christianity	628,999,900
Islam	554,700,200
Hinduism	463,815,200
Buddhism	247,587,500
Confucianism	150,964,000
Shinto	32,048,000
Taoism	20,056,000
Judaism	16,932,000

People have followed religions since ancient times. Scientists believe that the earliest religions were attempts by humans to explain things they did not understand. People believed that fire, storms, birth, and death were caused by *supernatural* forces—invisible forces caused by spirits or gods. They feared these forces and created ceremonies called *rituals* to honor them.

There are hundreds of religions in the world today. Those with the most followers include Judaism, Christianity, Islam, Hinduism, and Buddhism. The beliefs and practices of Hinduism took hundreds of years to develop. Each of the other four religions traces its beginnings to one person. Abraham founded Judaism. Jesus Christ began the Christian religion. Muhammad founded Islam, and Siddhartha Gautama founded Buddhism.

Religions such as Judaism and Christianity are *monotheistic*—they teach that there is one God. *Polytheistic* religions hold that there are a number of gods. The ancient Greeks and Romans followed polytheistic religions. They believed that several gods and goddesses influenced their lives. People who believe that God does not exist at all are called *atheists*. (*See* **gods and goddesses**.)

People worship God by praying or by attending religious ceremonies, called *services.* Some religions hold their services in great churches, temples, or mosques. People in many religions meet in small, simple buildings, homes, or meeting halls. Still others worship outdoors on riverbanks, in forests, or around a fire. No matter where they are held, these ceremonies help people celebrate important moments in their lives and the life of their religious community.

See also **Buddhism; Christianity; Hinduism; Islam;** and **Judaism.**

Rembrandt van Rijn

The Dutch painter Rembrandt van Rijn (REM-brant van RHINE) is often called one of the world's greatest artists. He painted scenes from the Bible, from history, and from everyday life. He also painted many *portraits*—pictures of people, including himself. His portraits showed what people looked like and what they felt. A glowing, golden light often falls on the subjects of his paintings.

Rembrandt was born in the city of Leiden in 1606. He studied with two artists. Around age 19, he started to paint on his own. He

Rembrandt painted this *self-portrait*— a picture of himself as a young man.

favored bright, intense colors and experimented with thick spots of paint, which he applied with a paintbrush handle.

Rembrandt was already well known when he moved to the Dutch capital city, Amsterdam, around 1631. Many of the city's important citizens had Rembrandt paint their portraits. He was so successful that he and his wife moved to a large house. But his happiness soon ended. Three of his children died, and in 1642, his wife died. After this, Rembrandt's paintings changed. He used dark colors and shadows more, and his paintings had more richness. His self-portraits showed sadness. His later paintings were not as popular as his earlier works had been. During the last years of his life, he painted mostly to please himself. Rembrandt died in 1669.

See also **painters and painting.**

Renaissance

The Renaissance was a period in European history when there was a rebirth of interest in the arts and sciences. The name *Renaissance* means "rebirth." The Renaissance lasted from about 1300 to 1600. The discoveries and ideas of this period completely changed the way people lived, worked, and thought.

The Renaissance began in Italy. Many Italian cities had become important trade centers. Besides goods for trade, people brought science and learning from Asia and the Middle East. Wealthy Italian bankers and merchants became *patrons*—supporters—of science and the arts. Another great influence that helped bring about the Renaissance was the discovery of the writings of the ancient Greeks and Romans. These earlier

Below, Renaissance architects built great domes such as the one on the cathedral in Florence, Italy. At right, a drawing of human anatomy was part of new scientific studies.

thinkers believed that people should develop all their talents and abilities.

During the Renaissance, writers, artists, and scientists looked at the world around them with fresh interest. Writers began writing books and poems in their native languages, instead of using Latin, as scholars and priests did. Artists painted scenes from nature and created lifelike sculptures of men and women. Great artists of this period included Leonardo da Vinci, Michelangelo, and Raphael. (*See* **Leonardo da Vinci; Raphael;** and **Michelangelo.**)

The Renaissance was a time of scientific discovery. People examined the human body and learned how blood circulates. Two inventions—the microscope and telescope—showed people new worlds. Copernicus, Galileo, and other scientists changed how people thought about physical forces on earth and in the heavens. (*See* **Copernicus, Nicolaus** and **Galileo.**)

The invention of movable type in the 1440s made it easier to print books. Printing presses were set up throughout Europe. This helped spread the ideas and discoveries of the Renaissance.

During this period, towns and cities grew, and many of the manors ruled by lords and small kingdoms united into nations.

People's curiosity about their world helped bring about the Age of Exploration. In the late 1400s, Europeans began to sail across the seas to find and explore new lands. (*See* **explorers.**)

By the 1600s, the new ideas of the Renaissance were part of everyday life. Many of these ideas still influence the way we look at our world.

Renoir, Pierre-Auguste

Renoir (re-NWAR) was a painter who tried to show the beauty of the world in his art. Renoir and many other painters of the late 1800s are known as *impressionists.* Impressionist paintings show things as they appeared at a certain moment to the artist.

A Girl With a Watering Can is one of Renoir's popular paintings.

Pierre-Auguste Renoir was born in 1841, in Limoges, France. At age 13, he went to work as a painter in a porcelain factory. At 21, he began to paint in the studio of another artist.

The paintings that Renoir showed in 1874 reflected his new ideas. He did not smoothly blend colors into each other. Instead, he painted small strokes of different colors side by side. When you look at these paintings, your eyes blend the colors together.

During the last 15 years of his life, Renoir lived in the south of France. He was a world-famous painter by this time. Although he had arthritis, a disease that makes it hard to move, he continued to paint. He also began to make models for sculptures. Renoir kept working until he died, in 1919, at the age of 78.

See also **painters and painting.**

The microscopic hydra (left) reproduces by dividing—a young hydra is breaking from the parent. Strawberry plants (right) may send out runners from which new plants grow.

reproduction

One way we can tell living things from non-living things is that living things can *reproduce* themselves. Plants produce seeds that grow into new plants. Fish and birds lay eggs in which their babies develop. Horses, dogs, and many other animals—including humans—give birth to live young. These are only a few of the ways in which living things reproduce.

Reproduction in Simple Living Things The simplest living things are *monerans* and *protists.* Most creatures in these two huge kingdoms have only one cell and are too small to be seen without a microscope. Most of these tiny living things reproduce *asexually*—they do not need to mate. Many reproduce simply by *fission*—separating into two parts. They multiply by dividing! Some reproduce in another way. A cell grows a small bump called a *bud.* This bud breaks off and grows into a cell like its parent.

Some protists—such as the paramecium—exchange some of their living material with another protist of the same kind before they break in two. This is called *conjugation.* (*See* **moneran** and **protist.**)

Living things in the *fungi* kingdom reproduce in another way. One fungus, the mushroom, lives underground most of the year. The part of a mushroom we see above the

ground is just the reproductive organ. This organ sheds tiny specks called *spores,* which are something like seeds. They can grow into new fungi if they land in a place with food and water. (*See* **fungus.**)

Reproduction in Plants Plants have several ways of reproducing. Simple plants, such as mosses and ferns, reproduce in two stages. One stage is asexual and the other is *sexual.* There are male and female branches of a moss. For the sexual stage of reproduction, sperm from the male branch must combine with eggs from a female branch. This is called *fertilization.* The fertilized egg grows into a form that is neither male nor female. This form produces spores by itself—asexually. When a spore finds moisture and nourishment, it grows into a new male or female form of the moss. Then the reproduction process begins again. (*See* **fern** and **mosses and liverworts.**)

The flowers of flowering plants are important for reproduction. *Pollen* from a male part of a flower must combine with an egg in the female part of a flower. Many plants rely on wind, insects, or birds to carry pollen from one flower to another of the same kind. When pollen and egg come together, a *seed* grows. The seed may be carried far from its parent plant. If it finds moisture and food, it will grow into a plant of the same kind. (*See* **flower; flowering plant;** and **seed.**)

Some flowering plants reproduce asexually as well as by producing seeds. For example, if you have eaten a strawberry, you know that there are seeds on the outsides of strawberries. But a strawberry plant may also send out a *runner*—a kind of stem that runs along the ground. Roots form at different spots along the runner and new plants grow. Plants that have bulbs, such as onions and tulips, may reproduce asexually from tiny bulbs that form around the base of the parent bulb.

Animal Reproduction   Nearly all animals reproduce only sexually. This means that sperm from a male and eggs from a female must come together to produce young.

Many female fish and amphibians lay thousands of eggs in the water. Males release sperm into the water, and some sperm unite with some of the eggs. Baby fish or amphibians grow from the fertilized eggs.

In many other animals, a male puts sperm into the female's body, where it unites with eggs. The females of most reptiles, birds, and insects lay fertilized eggs. Baby animals develop inside the eggs and then hatch.

In human beings and other mammals, a fertilized egg grows and develops inside the mother. When the baby has developed enough to live on its own, it is born alive. (*See* **birth.**)

Courtship   Many animals spend much time looking for and attracting a *mate.* This is called *courtship.*

A male and female grebe do a mating dance, lifting themselves nearly out of the water.

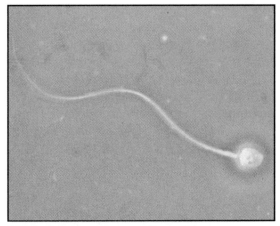

If this human sperm unites with a human egg, the egg becomes an *embryo*— the beginning of a human baby.

Some animals use sound to attract a mate. A male frog breathes in large amounts of air. Then he forces out the air across his vocal cords. This makes a loud croak. Female frogs hear the croak and go find him. Grasshoppers use sound, too. They make sounds by rubbing together parts of the body. Female mosquitoes attract males by the buzzing of their wings.

Some animals "dance," bobbing, hopping, and turning to attract a mate. Peacocks dance and fan out their beautiful tail feathers in the presence of peahens. Male sage grouse parade before the female grouse. Some butterflies and moths fly straight up, high into the sky.

Other animals attract mates by giving gifts. A male crow may give a stick to a female he is courting. A penguin may give a stone or a clump of snow.

Caring for the Young   Many animals protect their eggs until the young hatch. Most birds and mammals care for their babies after they hatch or are born. Parents feed and protect the babies. They teach them how to find food. Young swans stay with their parents for a year. Young camels stay with their mothers for four years. Young chimps stay with their mothers for almost ten years. Human children may stay with their parents for 18 years or more. Human parents care for their young longer than any other parents.

reptile

Lizards, snakes, turtles, tuataras, and alligators belong to a group of animals called reptiles. Reptiles are *vertebrates*—animals with backbones. A reptile has a skeleton made entirely of bone. A reptile has lungs and breathes air. Its body is covered with a dry, scaly skin. The skin prevents the animal from drying out. It also absorbs heat from the sun.

The word *reptile* comes from a Latin word meaning "to crawl." Most reptiles have four short legs and five clawed toes on each foot. Some, such as the snakes, do not have legs, but their ancestors had legs.

Most reptiles are *carnivores*—meat-eaters. They eat insects and small animals. Some turtles and lizards eat plants.

Reptiles are *cold-blooded*—their body temperature changes with the temperature of the environment. Reptiles die if their body temperature rises too high or falls too low. They have various ways to control their temperature. They are active when the weather is warm. They slow down when it is too cold or too hot. On a warm day, they may lie in the sun in the morning to warm up. When the sun gets too hot, they move into the shade. Some go into underground burrows when it is too cold or too hot aboveground.

Most reptiles lay eggs. The eggs are protected by thick, leathery shells. The eggs are laid in moist places on land. Reptiles that live in water, such as sea turtles, must come up on land to lay their eggs. Young reptiles look much like their parents, although they may have different colors. Some parents stay near their eggs and guard the young after they hatch. But most reptiles lay their eggs and then leave. When the young hatch, they must take care of themselves.

Reptiles are found in many environments—deserts, forests, marshes, streams, lakes, oceans, even people's gardens. The greatest number live in tropical and subtropical areas. It is too cold on high mountains and near the poles for most reptiles to live there.

Reptiles come in a great range of sizes. Pythons are among the largest. These snakes may be more than 8 meters (27 feet) long. Leatherback sea turtles may grow to 3 meters (10 feet) in length and weigh as much as 680 kilograms (1,500 pounds). The smallest reptiles are certain lizards that are only 2 centimeters (¾ inch) long.

Four Main Groups Reptiles have lived on earth for 300 million years. Many reptiles of the past were different from the reptiles of today. The best-known reptiles of long ago were the dinosaurs. These huge creatures dominated the world for millions of years. (*See* **dinosaur.**)

There are about 6,500 kinds of reptiles living today. Scientists place them in four groups. Crocodiles and alligators make up one group. In general, they are the largest of the reptiles. They have long bodies, powerful tails, and strong jaws.

Turtles and tortoises form a second group. Most have a hard shell around their body. When a turtle or tortoise is threatened, it pulls its head and legs inside the shell.

Lizards and snakes make up a third group. Usually, it is easy to tell these animals apart. Snakes are legless and cannot close their eyes. Most lizards have four legs and can shut their eyes.

Only one animal—the tuatara—belongs to the fourth group. This animal looks like a lizard. But there are important differences in the skull and teeth of the two groups.

Tuataras live only on islands off the coast of New Zealand. They are most active at

A gila monster is one of many reptiles that live in deserts.

dawn and in the early evening. They eat mostly insects, but they will also eat worms, snails, and lizards.

Some lizards and tuataras have a small hole covered by a thin layer of skin on top of their heads, above the eyes. This is sometimes called a *third eye*. The purpose of this structure is not known. It may sense light, but it does not see like a normal eye.

The dinosaur died out long ago. The other reptiles shown here are members of present-day reptile families.

skink, a lizard

tuatara

alligator

coral snake

brontosaurus

green turtle

Reptiles and People Some reptiles are very helpful. Snakes help farmers by eating mice and rats. Lizards feed on harmful insects. Freshwater turtles eat dead and sick fish, which helps keep the water clean.

Most reptiles are harmless. Some kinds of turtles, lizards, and small snakes make good pets. But some snakes and a lizard called the *Gila monster* are poisonous. Their bites can make people very sick or even kill them.

People hunt and kill many reptiles. They use the skins of crocodiles, alligators, lizards, and snakes for leather. They eat the flesh of snakes and turtles. Because of too much hunting, some of these animals are endangered. A few of them are protected by laws. (*See* **animals, endangered.**)

See also **alligators and crocodiles; snake; chameleon; lizard;** and **turtle.**

respiration

Respiration is the process of breathing in and out. When you sit quietly, you breathe in and out about 16 times each minute. When you breathe in, air goes into your lungs. When you breathe out, air leaves your lungs.

Respiration has two important functions. When you breathe air into your lungs, your blood takes oxygen from the air. At the same time, your blood gives up carbon dioxide, a waste product made by your body when you use energy. When you breathe out, the carbon dioxide leaves your body.

Your body uses oxygen you breathe in when it makes energy. You use this energy to work, play, and think. When you are quiet, your body does not need much energy. You breathe slowly. When you work and play hard, you need extra energy. You breathe faster and deeper. More oxygen gets into your blood, and your body is able to make the extra energy you need.

When your body makes energy, it also makes carbon dioxide. Your body cannot use this gas and must get rid of it. When you play hard and breathe fast, your body gets rid of extra carbon dioxide.

Animals breathe oxygen and give off carbon dioxide. Green plants take in carbon dioxide and give off oxygen.

All living things carry out respiration. Animals take in oxygen and breathe out carbon dioxide. For example, fish take oxygen from water through their gills and put carbon dioxide into the water. Insects breathe through special tubes on their sides. Plants use carbon dioxide to produce oxygen when they make their own food, during *photosynthesis*. In the daytime, while photosynthesis is going on, plants make enough oxygen for their own needs and release the rest into the air. But at night, plants take in oxygen and get rid of carbon dioxide through their leaves. (*See* **photosynthesis.**)

Each living cell—plant or animal—carries out respiration. *Cell respiration* takes place when a cell gets energy from food. The cells use oxygen and food to make energy. Food you eat has energy stored in it. During digestion, your body breaks the food into substances that can be carried by your blood and absorbed by your cells. Cells take these substances and break them down even more. When cells break down food, they release the energy stored in the food. This is the energy you use to do things. Oxygen has to be present for cells to release energy from food.

Respiration and cell respiration work together. Respiration brings in the oxygen that is needed for cell respiration, and it gets rid of the carbon dioxide that is produced by cell respiration.

See also **breathing.**

Revere, Paul

Paul Revere was an American patriot who warned the people of Lexington, Massachusetts, that British troops were coming. The story is told in Henry Wadsworth Longfellow's poem "Paul Revere's Ride."

Revere was born in Boston, Massachusetts, in 1735. The son of a silversmith, he learned his father's trade and later took over the family business. Revere was one of the patriots who dumped British tea into Boston Harbor in 1773. (*See* **Boston Tea Party.**)

In 1775, revolutionary leaders in Boston learned that British troops were planning to march on Concord. Revere arranged to signal the patriots with lanterns in a Boston church steeple. One lantern would mean the British were moving by land. Two would mean they were going by sea. Then, on the night of April 18, two lanterns burned in the North Church steeple. Revere rode to Lexington to warn of the British approach. Revere, William Dawes, and Dr. Samuel Prescott then galloped toward Concord, warning patriots along the way. Revere was captured by British scouts, but released. Later, he fought in the Revolutionary War.

When the war ended, Revere took up his trade as a silversmith again. By the time he died, in 1818, his fame as a craftsman was equal to his fame as a patriot.

See also **Revolutionary War.**

In April 1775, Paul Revere rode through the countryside near Boston, warning people that British troops would soon be there.

Revolutionary War

The Revolutionary War—also known as the War for Independence—was fought between Great Britain and its 13 American colonies. It began on April 19, 1775, and ended six and a half years later, on October 19, 1781. As a result of this war, the colonies became a free, self-governing nation—the United States of America.

Causes of the War The land along the east coast of North America belonged to Great Britain. It was divided into colonies, and the people there lived under British rule. The first successful British settlement in North America was Jamestown, Virginia, founded in 1607. After that, more settlers came. By 1733, there were 13 colonies and about 1 million people. (*See* **colonial life in America.**)

For most of this time, the British were busy fighting the French for control of land in North America. The American colonists meanwhile governed themselves. They elected many of their officials, made laws, and decided what taxes to pay.

When the French and Indian War ended, in 1763, Britain won most of France's land in North America. The French were no longer a threat, so Britain was able to pay more attention to the American colonies. That year, the British told the colonists that they could not settle the area between the Appalachian Mountains and the Mississippi River. Britain wanted to keep this land for the Indians. Many colonists were angry. They felt Britain was taking away their freedom of movement. (*See* **French and Indian War.**)

Britain had spent a great deal of money on the war against the French. The British prime minister, George Grenville, decided that the American colonists should help to pay some of Britain's debts. In 1764, the British Parliament passed the Sugar Act. This was a law that charged Americans a tax on molasses brought into the colonies. Parliament also passed the Quartering Act, which ordered Americans to feed and house

The British required a special stamp (left) on documents and paper. Colonists refused to buy the stamps (right).

British soldiers on duty in the colonies. The next year, Parliament passed the Stamp Act. Colonists had to buy tax stamps and put them on newspapers, legal documents, and playing cards.

The colonists angrily protested these laws. They joined secret groups—such as the Sons of Liberty—that tried to drive out the tax collectors. The colonists argued that since they were not represented in Parliament, Britain had no right to tax the colonists. They cried, "No taxation without representation!"

Alarmed by the protest, Parliament *repealed*—canceled—the Stamp Act. But a short time later, Parliament decided to tax glass, paper, lead, and tea shipped to the colonies. British soldiers were sent to make sure that these taxes were paid. On March 5, 1770, a crowd of colonists in Boston began making fun of the soldiers and threw snowballs at them. The soldiers fired into the crowd, killing five Americans. News of the "Boston Massacre" stirred up more anger at British rule.

In 1773, Parliament placed another tax on tea. Once again, Boston was the scene of rebellion. Late one night, members of the Sons of Liberty crept aboard British ships and threw more than 300 cases of tea into Boston Harbor. Parliament reacted to the "Boston Tea Party" by passing the *Intolerable Acts*—a series of harsh laws against Massachusetts. Boston Harbor was shut, making it difficult for people to get food and other goods. The colonial governor of Massachusetts was replaced by a British military governor. Public meetings could not be held without permission. An additional 10,000 British troops were sent to Massachusetts. (*See* **Boston Tea Party.**)

Steps Toward American Independence
News of these acts only united the colonies against Britain. In September 1774, representatives from 12 colonies met in Philadelphia to discuss American rights. The group—called the First Continental Congress—sent a message to the British king, George III, asking him to repeal the Intolerable Acts. If he did not, the Congress said, the colonists would refuse to buy British goods. The Congress also encouraged Massachusetts to form a *militia*—a small army—to resist British control. Militiamen, called Minutemen, began to train in the towns and villages across Massachusetts.

It was not long before the British military governor of Massachusetts, General Thomas

American soldiers fight on Breed's Hill in Boston in June 1775. They wounded many British soldiers, but finally gave up the hill when they ran out of ammunition.

Gage, learned about the militia. Spies told him that the Minutemen were hiding weapons and gunpowder in the village of Concord, outside of Boston. Gage ordered 800 British soldiers to capture the military supplies. A few colonists learned of the British plan. When the soldiers began their march from Boston on the night of April 18, 1775, Paul Revere, William Dawes, and Dr. Samuel Prescott rode out ahead of them to warn the Minutemen. (*See* **Revere, Paul.**)

By dawn of April 19, the British troops had reached the town of Lexington, on the way to Concord. On Lexington's village green, they found themselves face to face with a small number of Minutemen. Shots rang out, and seven Minutemen were killed. Another ten were wounded. The British marched on to Concord, where more Minutemen awaited them. Another battle followed, and the British turned back toward Boston. But the Minutemen hid along the road and killed 240 British soldiers.

Less than a month later, Vermont colonist Ethan Allen and his group of "Green Mountain Boys" moved against the British stronghold of Fort Ticonderoga in New York. Benedict Arnold and a small band of men had come from Massachusetts with the same idea. Allen and Arnold joined forces, and on May 10, 1775, they captured the fort. That same day, the Second Continental Congress met in Philadelphia. The Congress sent a message to King George, asking that Britain take no further steps against the American colonies. It also decided to organize an American army and named General George Washington as its commander. (*See* **Washington, George.**)

In June, the British attacked American forces at Breed's Hill, outside of Boston. The Americans had stationed men at Breed's Hill and at Bunker Hill, hoping to drive the British from Boston. The British lost over 1,000 men before forcing the Americans to retreat. In July 1775, Washington and his soldiers recaptured Boston from the British. (*See* **Bunker Hill.**)

Not all colonists wanted freedom from Britain. About one-third of them believed that if the king and Parliament would treat the colonies more fairly, the problem would be solved. These colonists were called *Tories* or *loyalists.* By June 1776, however, members of the Second Continental Congress decided that independence from Great Britain was the only possible course.

The Congress chose five of its members to write a declaration stating the colonies' reasons for breaking their ties with Britain. The declaration, written by Thomas Jefferson, was approved by the Congress on July 4, 1776. (*See* **Declaration of Independence.**)

Fighting the Revolutionary War The American soldiers were not experienced, and they were short of supplies and equipment. Because of this, the war at first went very badly for the colonists. Late in 1776, Washington and his troops took a bold action that encouraged the patriots. In the dark of Christmas night, they rowed across the icy Delaware River to a British camp at Trenton,

Washington visits troops at Valley Forge in the winter of 1777–1778. They were suffering from cold and hunger.

Revolutionary War

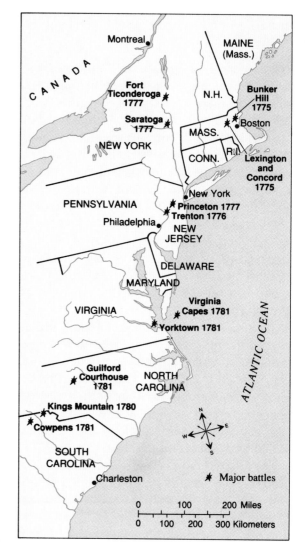

New Jersey. They attacked at sunrise, taking the British completely by surprise and capturing about 1,000 men. The Americans were also able to take much-needed weapons and supplies from the British.

In the fall of 1777, American and British forces clashed near Saratoga in New York. The Americans surrounded the enemy and forced General John Burgoyne to surrender, along with his 5,000 British troops. This great victory convinced other nations that the Americans might be able to win the war. France sent military aid to help the struggling Americans. A young French nobleman, the Marquis de Lafayette, even became a general in the American forces. (*See* **Lafayette, Marquis de.**)

During the winter of 1777 to 1778, Washington's army faced perhaps its worst period. Hungry, and lacking proper shelter and warm clothing, they camped out in the bitter cold of Valley Forge in Pennsylvania. At times, as many as half the men could not report for duty because they lacked socks, shoes, or coats. But over the winter, Washington's troops were given valuable combat training by Baron von Steuben, a German officer. (*See* **Valley Forge.**)

Following this harsh winter, things began to look better for the colonists. The new American navy was successfully attacking ships carrying supplies for the British forces. In 1779, Captain John Paul Jones won an important victory for America by capturing a heavily armed British warship. (*See* **Jones, John Paul.**)

In 1781, British troops marched to Yorktown, Virginia, near the Atlantic coast. American and French soldiers raced to surround the British force on land. Ships from the French fleet cut off any chance of British escape by sea. Trapped, General Charles Cornwallis and his British troops were forced to surrender. (*See* **Yorktown.**)

The British government was at last willing to talk about peace. American and British representatives met in Paris, and in 1783 a peace treaty was signed. Under the terms of the treaty, Britain gave up its claim to the American colonies. In addition, Britain gave the new United States all the land from the Atlantic Ocean to the Mississippi River and from Canada to Florida.

The Americans and French trapped the British at Yorktown (in distance). The British (in red uniforms) are giving up. This marked the end of the Revolution.

This Indian rhino has a thick, armorlike hide. Its horn is not yet fully grown.

rhinoceros

The rhinoceros, or "rhino," is the second-largest land mammal. Only the elephant is larger. The rhino has a large head and a stout body covered with a thick brownish or grayish hide. The hide has very little hair and is often wrinkled. The short legs have three toes. Each toe is encased in a hoof. A rhino has one or two pointed horns on top of its huge snout. These are not true horns. They are made of densely packed hair, not bone. Rhinos have small eyes and see poorly.

Rhinos eat grass and other plants. There are no sweat glands in a rhino's hide, so rhinos wallow in mud to cool off. The coating of dried mud protects the rhinos from the sun's heat.

Rhinos usually are very quiet and shy. But when cornered or angry, they can be very fierce. Lowering their heads so their horns face the attacker, they charge at speeds of up to 50 kilometers (30 miles) per hour.

There are five kinds of rhinos. Black and white rhinos live in Africa. Indian, Javan, and Sumatran rhinos live in Asia. The Indian rhinoceros is the largest kind of rhino, weighing up to 4,000 kilograms (8,800 pounds). The Sumatran is the smallest, usually weighing less than 1,000 kilograms (2,200 pounds).

Few rhinos are left on earth. Some kinds are nearly extinct. All five kinds are protected by law in their native lands.

Rhode Island

Capital: Providence
Area: 1,212 square miles (3,144 square kilometers) (smallest state)
Population (1980): 947,154 (1985): about 968,000 (42nd-largest state)
Became a state: May 29, 1790 (13th state)

Rhode Island is one of the six states that make up the region called New England, in the northeastern United States. It is bordered on the north and east by Massachusetts, on the west by Connecticut, and on the south by the Atlantic Ocean.

Land Rhode Island is by far the nation's smallest state. It is only about 48 miles (77 kilometers) from north to south and 37 miles (60 kilometers) from east to west. Narragansett Bay cuts almost all the way through it from north to south. The bay has more than 35 islands. The largest is called Rhode Island, like the state. The state also includes Block Island, 9 miles (14 kilometers) out in the Atlantic.

The land around Narragansett Bay is low and flat. It rises and becomes more hilly to the north and west. Breezes coming off the ocean and the bay keep Rhode Island from getting very hot in summer or very cold in winter.

History The first people to live in Rhode Island were Algonquian Indians. The first Europeans to visit Rhode Island may have been Norsemen, around the year 1000. Explorers from other European countries came in the 1500s and early 1600s.

The first major settlement was established in 1636 by Roger Williams, Rhode Island's founder. Williams had been living in Massachusetts. He had to leave because he did not agree with the religious ideas of the Puritans

who ruled Massachusetts. He believed that people should worship as they wished and that land should be bought, not taken, from the Indians. Williams named his settlement Providence, because he felt that God was watching over him. Soon he was joined by other people who wanted religious freedom, and more settlements grew up.

Like the Indians, the early colonists depended on the bay and the ocean for food. Fishing is still a major economic activity, and Rhode Island is second only to Maine and Massachusetts in the number of lobsters caught each year.

Newport, in the southern part of the island named Rhode Island, became a very busy port. It was a center for the whaling industry. Newport was also deeply involved in the slave trade in the 1700s. At that time, ships filled with rum would leave Newport and other Narragansett Bay harbors. They would sail to the west coast of Africa, where the rum would be traded for slaves. Then the ships would sail back across the Atlantic to the West Indies, where the slaves would be sold for huge profits. The ships would pick up molasses in the West Indies. Back in Rhode Island, it would be made into rum, which was traded for more slaves.

In the early 1800s, a series of wars and other problems stopped trade for a while and kept ships home. Wealthy Rhode Islanders, unable to make money in shipping and trade, began to develop the state's industries. With plenty of waterpower and workers, the state soon was known for manufacturing.

The nation's first successful waterpowered cotton mill was built in Rhode Island in the 1790s. By the middle 1800s, 153 mills were busy spinning cotton thread and weaving cloth. Most of the textile industry has since moved to the southern United States, but textiles are still Rhode Island's leading industry. Half of the lace made in the United States is made in Rhode Island.

Other industries that developed in the 1800s were costume jewelry, sterling silverware, machinery, and machine tools.

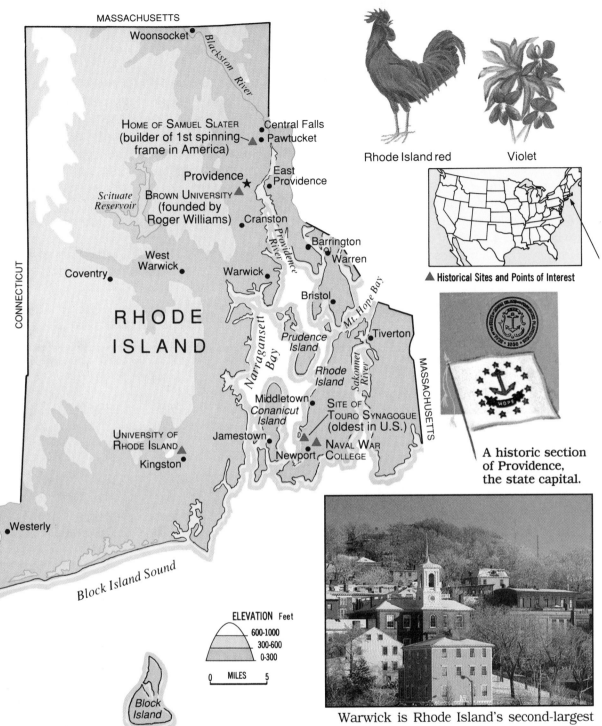

MASSACHUSETTS

Woonsocket

Blackston River

HOME OF SAMUEL SLATER
(builder of 1st spinning
frame in America)

Central Falls
Pawtucket

Providence

East
Providence

BROWN UNIVERSITY
(founded by
Roger Williams)

Scituate
Reservoir

Cranston

Barrington

Warren

West
Warwick

Warwick

Coventry

Providence River

R H O D E
I S L A N D

CONNECTICUT

Bristol

Narragansett Bay

Mt. Hope Bay

Prudence
Island

Tiverton

Rhode
Island

Sakonnet River

MASSACHUSETTS

Middletown
Conanicut
Island

UNIVERSITY OF
RHODE ISLAND

Jamestown

SITE OF
TOURO SYNAGOGUE
(oldest in U.S.)

NAVAL WAR
COLLEGE

Kingston

Newport

Westerly

Block Island Sound

ELEVATION Feet

600-1000
300-600
0-300

0   MILES   5

Block
Island

Rhode Island red

Violet

▲ Historical Sites and Points of Interest

A historic section
of Providence,
the state capital.

Warwick is Rhode Island's second-largest city. It lies south of Providence on Narragansett Bay. Warwick was once a textile-manufacturing town known for the making of lace. Now it is a trading center.

Pawtucket, in the northern part of the state, is noted for making machinery and machine tools, rubber products, lace, and cotton and woolen textiles.

Newport is a vacation spot for wealthy Americans and holds many yacht races.

People There are more people per square mile in Rhode Island than in any other state except New Jersey. Many live in Providence, Rhode Island's capital and largest city. It is an industrial, commercial, educational, and transportation center. The principal industry in Providence is textile manufacturing. It is also a leader in manufacturing costume jewelry and silverware.

rhyme

Words that rhyme sound alike—their sounds echo each other. *House* and *mouse* rhyme. So do *season* and *reason*. Rhyming words add to the beautiful sound and rhythm of many poems. A short, simple poem that uses rhyming words is also called a *rhyme.* "Little Miss Muffet sat on a tuffet" is a line from a popular children's nursery rhyme. (*See* **Mother Goose.**)

In *perfect rhymes,* the endings of the two words sound exactly alike. *Red* and *head* rhyme perfectly. *Imperfect rhymes* sound almost alike. *Together* and *gather* are examples of imperfect rhymes. Some words, such as *water* and *later,* only look as though they should rhyme.

Rhymes are called *masculine* and *feminine,* depending on which of the syllables in the words rhyme. If only the last syllables echo in both words, then the rhyme is masculine. *Hairy* and *busy* make a masculine rhyme. When the last two or three syllables echo, the rhyme is feminine. *Hairy* and *dairy* make a feminine rhyme.

See also **poetry.**

rhythm

Rhythm is one of the main elements of music. The others are melody and harmony. (*See* **melody** and **harmony.**)

An easy way to understand rhythm is to listen to the drums in a marching band. They beat out a rhythm for the band to march to. Rhythm is also important in jazz and rock music. In a jazz group, the rhythm section includes drums, a string bass, and perhaps other instruments, such as a piano.

Rhythm has two parts. The first, called *meter,* is the main rhythm. A march has a meter of twos—ONE-two-ONE-two-ONE-two. People can easily march to the beat—LEFT-right-LEFT-right-LEFT-right. But in a waltz or a minuet, the rhythm moves in threes—ONE-two-three-ONE-two-three. This is a good dance rhythm. (*See* **dance.**)

The meter of a piece of written music is shown at the very beginning in the *time signature.* If it says 2/4, there are two beats to each measure. The piece may be a march. The marking 3/4 means three beats to the measure. The piece may be a waltz.

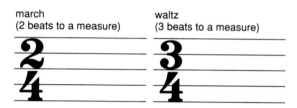

march
(2 beats to a measure)

waltz
(3 beats to a measure)

The second part of rhythm is the amount of time each note is played. In written music, this time is shown by how a note looks. In 4/4 time, the different notes have these values:

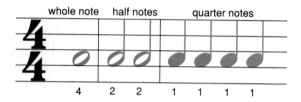

whole note   half notes   quarter notes

Sometimes we can recognize a song just by seeing the rhythm of the first few notes. For example, one song that begins

Oh—   say can you   see?

is "The Star Spangled Banner," the American national anthem.

Rhythm is also an important part of poetry. Many poems in English have four *feet* in each line. A foot usually has one unstressed sound and one stressed sound. Here is an example:

Be**side** the **lake,** be**neath** the **trees,**
Fluttering and **danc**ing **in** the **breeze.**

Other poems may have very different rhythms. (*See* **poetry.**)

rice

Rice is the main food for about half of the world's people. Rice plants belong to the grass family and are called *cereal grains.* Rice is related to oats, wheat, and barley.

People in China, India, and other countries of Asia grow and eat most of the world's rice. Many Asians eat rice at every meal. Often the rice is flavored with small amounts of vegetables, fish, or meat.

Rice grows best in ground that is flooded or where there is a lot of rain. In many parts of the world, people use simple tools to plant rice on small farms. Most of the rice produced in the United States is grown on large farms and gathered by machine.

Rice seeds are planted in a dry or damp field. After the seeds have sprouted, the farmer floods the field, or moves the young plants to a flooded field. A flooded rice field is called a *paddy.* As the plants grow, a *head* develops at the end of each tall stem. The head contains from 50 to 300 flowers. The grains of rice develop from the flowers. While the grains are ripening, up to 6 inches (15 centimeters) of water remains on the paddy. The farmer drains the water shortly before harvesting the rice.

In many countries, farmers use knives to harvest the stalks of rice. The stalks are then bundled and allowed to dry. Next, the grains of rice are separated from the stalks by a process called *threshing.* In most Asian countries, people thresh rice by beating the bundles against hard objects until the grains drop from the stalks. On larger farms, machines called *combines* harvest and thresh rice at the same time.

A grain of rice has a brown covering called a *hull.* The hull can be removed by machine or by hand. Underneath the hull is another brown coating called the *bran.* The bran contains most of the grain's vitamins, minerals, and oils. *Brown rice* has the bran. *White rice* has had the bran removed. Some of the vitamins and minerals that were lost with the bran are often added to white rice.

Wild rice—sometimes called *Indian rice* or *Canada rice*—is not really rice at all. It is the grain from a kind of grass that grows naturally in shallow parts of lakes and rivers, but does not grow well on farms.

People probably started growing rice thousands of years ago in Asia. Today in the United States, Arkansas, California, Texas, and Louisiana are the four leading rice-growing states.

Below, rice grows in *paddies*—flooded fields. At right, the parts of a grain of rice.

Rio de Janeiro

Rio de Janeiro—Rio, for short—is Brazil's second-largest city and its cultural center. It rests on the southeastern coast of Brazil, and is almost surrounded by mountains. Much of the city is built on hills, and part of it faces the Atlantic Ocean. Most of the city is on or near the western shore of Guanabara Bay—one of the largest and most beautiful bays in the world. According to tradition, Portuguese explorers entered the bay in January 1502, thinking the bay was the mouth of a large river. So they named the area Rio de Janeiro—"River of January" in Portuguese. Rio's most famous mountain, Sugarloaf, sits on a strip of land that forms part of the entrance to Guanabara Bay.

Rio is a mix of gleaming white modern buildings and small brown houses built when Brazil was a Portuguese colony. Luxury apartment houses line the Copacabana and other popular beaches. Palm trees grow along the city's wide streets. Yet on the hillsides surrounding the city, there are *favelas* —shacks where many thousands of the city's poor people live.

Sugarloaf Mountain overlooks an inviting harbor and beach in Rio.

Rio's main business is tourism and recreation. People from all over the world come to Rio to enjoy its restaurants and nightclubs, fine beaches, and beautiful setting. The entire city celebrates during Carnival—a festival held each year before Lent begins. For three days, the *Cariocas*—the people of Rio—sing, dance, and parade through the streets in colorful costumes. The city fills with thousands of visitors.

Rio is also an important center for banking and industry. Factories in and around the city make clothing, shoes, tires, chemicals, and other products. Rio's seaport is one of the busiest in South America. It is from here that Brazilian goods—such as coffee, sugar, and iron ore—are exported to other countries. More goods enter Brazil through Rio de Janiero than through any other port.

The city of Rio was founded by the Portuguese in 1565. It was a small village at first. It began to grow at the end of the 1600s, when gold was discovered nearby. By 1763, it was the largest city in Portugal's Brazilian colony, and was made the capital. In 1822, Rio became the capital of the newly independent nation of Brazil. It remained the capital until 1960, when the city of Brasília became the capital.

Rio Grande

The Rio Grande is one of the world's longest rivers. It is 1,885 miles (3,016 kilometers) long. It is an important source of water for drinking and irrigation in the southwestern United States and northern Mexico. But most of the river is too shallow for large boats.

The Rio Grande begins high up in the Rocky Mountains of Colorado and flows south through New Mexico. Near El Paso, Texas, the Rio Grande begins flowing southeastward, forming 1,300 miles (2,080 kilometers) of the border between the United States and Mexico. It empties into the Gulf of Mexico just beyond Brownsville, Texas, and Matamoros, Mexico.

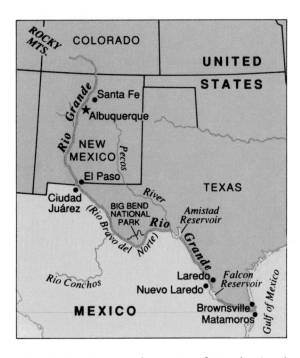

Rivers run downhill toward the sea. They receive water from smaller rivers and streams called *tributaries*.

Irrigation has made much of the dry land beside the Rio Grande useful for farming and ranching. In Colorado, cattle ranches and potato farms are on both sides of the Rio Grande. In Texas, the river has formed a wide, fertile coastal plain. Citrus fruits, onions, and sugar beets grow well there. In New Mexico, the river has cut deep canyons.

Pueblo Indians have lived and farmed along the Rio Grande for hundreds of years. Spanish priests arrived from Mexico early in the 1600s. They established missions and gave the river and many nearby places Spanish names.

river

A river is a large, long body of flowing water. Streams, too, are flowing bodies of water, but they are smaller than rivers. The place where a river begins is called its *source*. A river's source may be a lake, a glacier, or even just snow high up in the mountains.

A stream that flows into another stream or a river is called a *tributary*. As more tributaries flow into a river, more water is added to its flow. The world's longest rivers—the Nile, Amazon, Mississippi, and Volga—have many tributaries.

A river and its tributaries carry off the water that falls as rain or snow on a certain area of land. This area is called the river's *drainage basin*. You can find the boundary of a drainage basin along the tops of a range of hills or mountains. This boundary is called a *divide*. The water on one side of the divide runs downhill in one direction. On the other side, the water runs off in the opposite direction.

The divide in the Rocky Mountains—the *continental divide*—is higher than any other in North America. East of the continental divide, rivers run to the Gulf of Mexico and the Atlantic Ocean. West of the divide, they run to the Pacific and the Arctic oceans. (*See* **continental divide**.)

In North America, the drainage basins east of the continental divide are much larger than the basins west of the divide. East of the divide, the area drained by the Mississippi and Missouri rivers is over 2.5 million square kilometers (1 million square miles). This is the third-largest river basin in the world, after the basins of the Amazon River and the Congo in Africa. West of the divide, the Columbia River basin is the largest. It covers less than 1.3 million square kilometers (500,000 square miles).

The Water Cycle Most rivers carry water from their drainage basins to the sea. A giant river, such as the Mississippi or Amazon, carries hundreds of thousands of gallons to

When rivers flow through gently sloping land, they twist and turn, forming curves called *meanders*.

the sea each day. But nature has a way of returning water from the sea to the land.

Heat from the sun causes some seawater to *evaporate*—turn into a gas called *water vapor*. The water vapor rises in the atmosphere. High up, where it is colder, the water vapor cools. This causes it to *condense*—become a liquid again. You see this liquid as clouds. When winds blow the clouds over land, the water falls as rain or snow. Again, the water drains into rivers that flow to the sea. We call this movement of water between atmosphere and the earth the *water cycle*. Without it, life would not be possible on earth. (*See* **water cycle.**)

Rivers and Erosion As rivers rush down mountains and flow across plains, they *erode* the land—wear away soil and rocks. Some rivers have carved deep canyons in the rocks of plateaus. The Colorado River began to erode what is now the mile-deep Grand Canyon about 6 million years ago.

Rivers also carry away the soil and rocks from the land they erode. Once in the river, this soil and rock is called *sediment*. A big river can carry tons of sediment. The water may have so much sediment in it that it looks muddy. At the river's *mouth* the place where it meets the sea—the river slows down. Slow-moving water cannot carry as

much sediment, so most of the sediment settles to the bottom. This eventually creates a *delta*—a fan shaped land area at the mouth of a river.

Heavy rains and snow may swell a river and make it too full for its *channel*—the wide groove it has cut into the land. When the river floods, water pours over the *floodplain*—the flat land alongside the river.

Floodwaters can do a great deal of damage on the floodplain. They may cover fields, rotting the crops. They may cover roads and rail lines, making it impossible for cars and trains to move. They may flood houses, forcing people to leave their homes.

But not all of what happens during a flood is terrible. During a flood, the river drops tons of sediment on the floodplain. With each flood, another layer of sediment is deposited. This makes the soil rich and fertile. Farmers can grow good crops on this soil year after year. (*See* **flood.**)

Rivers and People People have always chosen to build their towns and cities along rivers. The rivers provide water for irrigation and sometimes drinking water, too. Rivers are important for transportation and trade. Today, we use the water power of rivers to produce electric power. We also use rivers for recreation—sailing and sport fishing.

A dam can help prevent flooding downstream, can store water for use in dry seasons, and can help make electricity. People swim, boat, or fish in the lake behind the dam.

But heavy use by humans has been very bad for some rivers. In many western states, taking too much water from rivers for irrigation has done great damage to delicate river ecosystems. Many rivers are now too polluted to produce fish for food, and some are too polluted even to swim in. Companies and towns have dumped wastes in the rivers. The government has passed laws to help protect our rivers. Environmental groups are working to help clean up our rivers and preserve them. (*See* **environment** and **water pollution**.)

See also **canyon; delta; erosion;** and **evaporation**.

road, *see* **highway**

Rivers provide important routes for freight. This big ocean-going container ship is sailing up the Savannah River in Georgia, helped by a smaller tugboat.

roadrunner

The roadrunner is a bird that rarely flies. Most of the time, it runs. Roadrunners can run very fast. They depend on running to escape from enemies and to catch their food—insects, lizards, and other speedy animals. Roadrunners are daring, too. They even eat young rattlesnakes!

Roadrunners live in deserts in the southwestern United States and northern Mexico. When people first built roads through the deserts, there were no cars. People rode horses. Roadrunners got their name because they liked to run alongside the horses. Today, roadrunners sometimes try to run alongside cars. But they cannot run as fast as cars.

The roadrunner is a member of the cuckoo family. It is about 60 centimeters (2 feet) long, including its long tail. The tail usually points up. The bird uses its tail and its short wings to keep its balance while running.

The roadrunner is a bird that runs more than it flies.

The female roadrunner builds a large nest of twigs high in a cactus, tree, or shrub. The two parents take turns sitting on the eggs. When the babies hatch, they do not have any feathers. The parents care for the babies until they have feathers and are ready to leave the nest.

Robin Hood

Robin Hood is a figure from English legend. He was an outlaw, but to the common

Robin Hood, hero of many legends, lived in Sherwood Forest in England.

people, he was a hero. He was said to steal from the rich and give to the poor. Robin Hood would not kill the people he robbed unless they tried to kill him first. He loved Maid Marian, a noble lady, and protected all women. He was considered the best English archer. He could shoot any target with his bow and arrow.

Robin Hood's gang was called the "Merry Men of Sherwood Forest," after the woods in which they lived. One of the most famous Merry Men was Friar Tuck, a fat, good-hearted priest. Another was Little John, a giant who was over 7 feet (2.1 meters) tall. The sheriff of Nottingham was Robin Hood's enemy. He wanted Robin hanged.

What we know of Robin Hood comes mostly from songs called *ballads*. Some date back to the 1300s. We do not know who wrote the words or how the melodies went. Many tell of Robin's adventures.

One well-known ballad is called "Robin Hood and Guy of Gisborne." It tells how Little John was captured by the sheriff of Nottingham. Robin won a fight with Guy of Gisborne—a friend of the sheriff's. Robin took Guy's clothes and put them on. The sheriff was fooled into thinking that Robin was Guy and told him to kill Little John. Instead, Robin set his friend free. As soon as the sheriff and his men saw Little John and Robin Hood ready to fight, they fled.

Some scholars think a real Robin Hood may have existed. Someone named Robertus Hood is mentioned in records from 1230. He is called an outlaw. Other writers think Robin Hood was the earl of Huntingdon, since the earl's name was Robert Fitzooth, and he was born in 1160 in Nottingham.

Robin Hood appears in Sir Walter Scott's famous novel *Ivanhoe,* printed in 1819. In it, Robin and Friar Tuck help Ivanhoe and other Englishmen fight the Normans. Here, Robin Hood is seen as an English nobleman holding out against the Normans, warriors who invaded England in 1066.

See also **English writers.**

Robinson, Jackie

Jackie Robinson was a baseball star with the Brooklyn Dodgers. He made history in 1947 when he became the first black person to play on a major-league baseball club.

Robinson was born in Georgia in 1919. At that time, black athletes were forbidden to play on major-league baseball teams. Instead, they played in separate leagues called the Negro leagues. Robinson began as a star football player at the University of California at Los Angeles. He was a talented star of baseball's Negro leagues when the Dodgers' general manager, Branch Rickey, signed him to play baseball in Brooklyn, New York.

Other players and teams were angry. But baseball commissioner Ford Frick stood up for Robinson's right to play. Robinson opened the doors of major-league baseball to blacks. Many other players from the Negro leagues later joined the teams of the American and National leagues.

Robinson played for ten years in the major leagues and led the Dodgers to the World Series six times. He was named the National

Jackie Robinson was the first black player to play modern major-league baseball.

League's most valuable player in 1949. In 1962, Robinson was elected to baseball's Hall of Fame.

robot

A robot is a machine that does mechanical tasks in a human way. Many people think all robots are like the ones they see in movies—humanlike beings with stiff metal limbs and flashing lights. In fact, many robots do

This robot is used to handle dangerous radioactive wastes.

Above, robots help to assemble cars.
They do a few jobs over and over.
At right, robot "waiters" serve food.

not look like human figures at all. A robot may be simply a box with a mechanical arm or hand.

The work of designing robots to perform tasks is called *robotics*. People plan the robot's movements and then program a computer to guide the robot in these movements. Once a program is written for a certain task—such as welding an automobile door or painting a wall—the program may be run again and again. The robot will repeat the job in exactly the same way all day long.

Some robots are equipped with cameralike "eyes." Their computers are programmed to compare what the robots "see" with pictures stored in their computer memory. This way a robot can recognize objects it needs to use. Some computer programs allow robots to choose between one tool and another, or objects of certain colors or sizes.

More and more factories are using robots to perform tasks that used to be done by people. New factories are built so robots can do most of the work. There are many reasons why factories prefer to use robots for some jobs. Robots can perform boring tasks without losing interest and becoming careless. They can perform complicated tasks without making mistakes. They can handle dangerous materials and jobs without the risk of getting hurt or sick. Simple changes in computer programs allow robots to switch from one job to another quickly and easily. Having a robot do the work costs less than having a person do the work. But robots cannot replace humans. Robots cannot think for themselves or handle any problems they have not been programmed to handle.

Of the thousands of robots in the world today, most are used in factories. But robots can be used in other places, too. They are used in space exploration. A robot in a large office in Washington, D.C., picks up and delivers mail. Other robots direct traffic. Robots are used to imitate sickness so medical students can learn to recognize the illness and try out a cure. Some armies are studying how robots might be used in war.

rock

Rock is the hard, solid material that makes up the earth's *crust*—its outer shell. Rocks are important in the work of *geologists*—scientists who study the earth and its history.

If you live on a flat, level plain, chances are that the only rock you can find for miles around is in the form of small, smooth, rounded stones. Most of the rock in your area is buried deep below the ground, under a thick blanket of soil, sand, and clay. This solid layer of rock is called *bedrock*.

If you live where there are hills and valleys, cliffs and canyons, the bedrock may be so close to the surface that it pokes up in places. A place where the bedrock is on the surface is called an *outcrop*.

Geologists study outcrops to find out what kind of bedrock lies beneath the surface. They use a rock hammer to chip away samples from an outcrop. Then they look at the chips under a magnifying glass or microscope to see what kind of minerals are in the rock. A geologist can tell from the minerals how the rock was formed. (*See* **mineral.**)

There are three kinds of rock—*igneous, sedimentary,* and *metamorphic.* Each kind forms in its own way.

Igneous Rock Igneous rocks form from cooled *magma*—melted rock material that is deep within the earth. As magma rises toward the earth's surface, it cools. If it cools enough before reaching the surface, it turns into a rock such as granite. If the magma is still hot and liquid when it reaches the surface, it pours out or shoots up as lava. As the lava cools, it becomes solid *volcanic rock,* such as basalt or pumice.

Sedimentary Rock Sedimentary rocks form on or near the surface of the earth. Some sedimentary rocks begin to form on the bottom of a large body of water, such as a lake or sea. The streams and rivers that empty into these bodies of water bring with them tiny pieces of rock and mineral. Depending on what size they are, these little bits collect together to make clay, mud, silt, or sand.

Sediments such as clay, mud, silt, and sand can pile up to form thick layers. Over millions of years, these layers become buried by newer sediments, and the older sediments gradually turn to rock. Water seeps through the sediments, and minerals that are dissolved in the water are left in the tiny spaces between the grains of sediment. These minerals act as a natural cement to hold the grains together. Shale, siltstone, and sandstone are examples of sedimentary rocks that form this way. Shale is formed from layers of clay. Siltstone is formed from silt. Sandstone is formed from sand.

Limestone, another kind of sedimentary rock, forms from the skeletons of small sea

Geologists learn much about rocks from rock *outcrops* like this one in Wyoming.

TYPES OF ROCKS

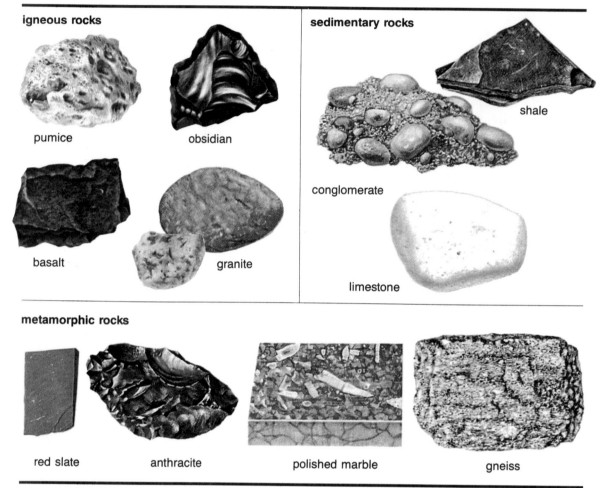

igneous rocks

pumice

obsidian

basalt

granite

sedimentary rocks

shale

conglomerate

limestone

metamorphic rocks

red slate

anthracite

polished marble

gneiss

creatures called *plankton.* As the plankton die, their tiny skeletons fall to the bottom of the sea. Gradually, they form a thick blanket of sediment. Like the other kinds of sediment, when this deposit becomes buried, it turns to rock.

Not all sedimentary rocks are formed from sediments deposited on the bottom of seas and lakes. Dry sediments can become buried and turn to rock. One example of such sediment is the sand that piles up in desert dunes. Geologists looking at certain kinds of sandstone see long, curved lines. They know these lines were made by wind blowing across sand dunes. Sandstone with these lines is called *cross-bedded.*

Sedimentary rocks provide stone for building. They also contain most of the world's remaining deposits of oil, gas, and coal.

Metamorphic Rock Sometimes sedimentary rock, such as limestone, becomes deeply buried. The earth's heat and pressure slowly change it to a new rock—marble. Such a rock is called *metamorphic.* It has *metamorphosed*—changed. The difference between this new, metamorphic rock and its parent limestone is that the tiny skeletons of plankton have been changed into crystals of a mineral called *calcite.*

When sandstone, a sedimentary rock, is buried, it changes into a hard, shiny metamorphic rock called *quartzite.* When shale is metamorphosed, it becomes *slate*—the hard, dark gray rock from which blackboards and shingles are made.

Igneous rocks can also be changed by heat and pressure. When an igneous rock such as granite is metamorphosed, it may change

90

into a rock with layers of dark and light minerals. Such a rock is called *gneiss*. Other igneous rocks may metamorphose to *schist*—a dark rock made of small, shiny flakes of black minerals and mica.

See also **geology; earth history; granite; mica; sand;** and **sandstone.**

rocket

The rocket is one of the simplest yet most powerful of all engines. It has no moving parts, but it can propel things at great speeds. Rockets are used to send spacecraft into space and to send satellites high enough to go into orbit. Rockets carry scientific instruments far into space. Small rockets are used to launch fireworks. Rockets can also carry explosives and be used as weapons.

A rocket is a tube that is open at one end and closed at the other. Fuel and oxygen are fed into the tube. The oxygen makes the fuel burn furiously. Exhaust gases from the burning fuel rush out from nozzles at the rear of the rocket. This propels the rocket forward at high speed, just as air rushing out of a balloon sends it flying in the opposite direction. (*See* **jet engine.**)

A rocket's *payload* is what it carries. The payload can be a weapon, a television satellite, Fourth of July fireworks, or space explorers from Earth. Many rockets that have weapons as their payloads are guided to their targets. Rockets of this kind are called *guided missiles.* They may be guided by computer, laser, or heat. (*See* **missile.**)

History Nearly 800 years ago, the Chinese were launching rockets with tubes made of bamboo and paper. The rocket's *casing*—tube—was filled with fast-burning chemical powders. It also held chemicals that released oxygen. As the chemicals burned, gases were produced. Gases shooting from the rocket drove it forward. The Chinese used their rockets mostly for launching fireworks. They also used rockets as weapons. The flight path of these rockets was set by aiming them before launching,

A rocket blasts off from the
Kennedy Space Center in Florida.

much as an arrow is aimed. Tail fins, like feathers on arrows, kept the rockets flying straight.

Marco Polo and other travelers brought the rocket to Europe around the year 1300. Over the centuries, people developed larger and more powerful rockets. Metal casings replaced the bamboo-and-paper casings used by the Chinese. Metal casings did not burn along with the burning fuel. They did not explode as easily as the bamboo-and-paper casings from the great force of the exhaust gases. Rockets used in war had explosives added to their tips.

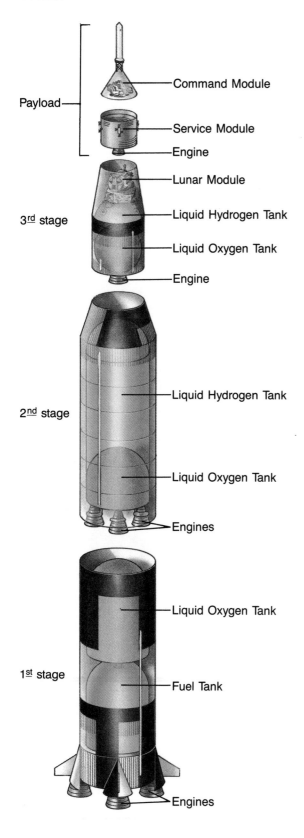

Payload

Command Module

Service Module

Engine

3rd stage

Lunar Module

Liquid Hydrogen Tank

Liquid Oxygen Tank

Engine

2nd stage

Liquid Hydrogen Tank

Liquid Oxygen Tank

Engines

1st stage

Liquid Oxygen Tank

Fuel Tank

Engines

Liquid-Fuel Rockets Until the 1900s, all rockets used *solid fuel*—chemical powders. In 1926, Robert H. Goddard, a rocket scientist, invented a rocket that burned liquid fuels, such as alcohol. Instead of carrying chemicals to release oxygen, most liquid-fuel rockets carry a supply of liquid oxygen.

The Germans used liquid-fuel rockets during World War II. Their V-2 rockets traveled about 5,760 kilometers (3,600 miles) per hour. That is 1 mile per second—more than four times the speed of sound! The V-2s were launched from Germany to hit English cities 800 kilometers (500 miles) or more away. A V-2's flight path took it 110 kilometers (70 miles) above the earth.

In the 1950s, the U.S. military experimented with airplanes that had rocket engines. Some of these, such as the X-15, set speed and height records for airplanes. Today, the military is studying ways to make rocket planes that would also be able to travel in space.

Multistage Rockets The V-2 was a *single-stage rocket.* All of its fuel and oxygen were contained in one section of the rocket. Goddard developed liquid-fuel rockets with more than one stage.

A *multistage rocket* has two or more stages. The powerful first stage—the *booster*—lifts the rocket from the launchpad. The booster fires for less than a minute, but it supplies hundreds of thousands of pounds of *thrust*—pushing power. It lifts the entire rocket off the launchpad and thousands of feet into the air. Once the fuel in the booster is burned, this first stage drops off, and the second stage fires. The rocket engine in the second stage is not as powerful as the booster, since it has less to lift. After the second stage drops off, the third stage has even less to lift.

To escape the pull of the earth's gravity, a rocket must reach a speed of at least 40,000 kilometers (25,000 miles) per hour—seven times the speed of the V-2 rocket. Only a multistage rocket can reach such a high speed. (*See* **space exploration.**)

A rock band in concert uses brilliant lights to help create excitement.
Sounds from voices and instruments are fed into a powerful sound system.

rock music

Rock music is a type of American music that first became popular in the 1950s. Rock music has a strong, lively beat that makes people feel like dancing. Usually, the music uses a few harmonies or *chords,* repeating them several times in the same song. The words of rock music are often about the concerns of young people. They may be about love or about the way young people get along with their friends, parents, and teachers.

The most important instrument in rock music is the electric guitar. A rock band may also include a piano or an electric keyboard, a string bass (often electrified), drums, and a synthesizer. A rock band may use many other instruments, too. Often, a lead singer sings the verses of the songs. The rest of the group sings the choruses while they play their instruments. Amplifiers increase the volume of the sound.

History One of the earliest successful rock bands was Bill Haley and the Comets. Their song "Rock Around the Clock" was used in a film called *Blackboard Jungle,* about a big-city school. The song became popular throughout the United States and Europe in the middle 1950s.

The first great rock star was singer Elvis Presley. His recordings became big hits in 1956 and 1957. Two of his early hits were "Heartbreak Hotel" and "Hound Dog." Soon he was appearing on television and in movies. His fans continue to worship him, years after his death in 1977.

Presley brought together several styles of music. One of these was country music, popular among whites in the South. Another was the music of black performers, known as rhythm and blues.

The recordings of early rock stars were played in many parts of the world. Soon, other countries had their own rock musicians. In the 1960s, several British rock groups became world-famous.

The most popular of the British groups was the Beatles. In the middle 1960s, they toured the United States, thrilling audiences wherever they went. Two of the Beatles, John Lennon and Paul McCartney, wrote most of their songs. They brought many new ideas into rock. Their songs were more complicated than earlier rock songs had been. They relied less on a heavy beat and used more complex harmonies. Many Beatles songs, such as "Yesterday" and "All You Need Is Love," are still heard today.

Elvis Presley (left) was one of the first stars of rock music. The Beatles (right) were a British rock group that helped make rock popular around the world.

The Beatles broke up in 1970, but they continued to perform as individuals. In 1980, John Lennon was shot and killed by a crazed fan in New York City.

The Rolling Stones, led by Mick Jagger, was another popular rock group from England. Many of their songs were angry and critical of society.

Another important development during the 1960s was the blending of folk and rock music. Bob Dylan was among the most successful folk rock performers. His songs expressed strong opinions about social issues.

Rock music was also used in many shows and musicals. *Hair* was the first successful rock musical on Broadway. The popular rock musical *Jesus Christ Superstar* had a religious message.

While rock was popular in recordings, some groups put on spectacular live performances for audiences in sports arenas or football stadiums. They used bright colored lights and huge speakers to entertain and excite their audiences. In the 1970s, more rock musicians performed in elaborate costumes and makeup. Some rock musicians danced while they sang and played, which made their performances—and their audiences—even livelier.

In the 1980s, the music video began showing up on cable television. In a video, top rock stars perform their hit songs. Sometimes the stars are shown playing, singing, and dancing. Other videos use experimental video techniques to tell a story or describe a mood that is related to the music. Some performers, such as Michael Jackson and Madonna, became international stars because of their videos.

In the 1950s, when Haley's Comets and Elvis Presley first became popular, many people believed that rock music was a fad. They thought that within a year or two, it would disappear. But rock has grown and changed over the years. It continues to blend music from different lands and cultures. In some rock music today, you can hear the influence of music from Africa and the West Indies. Rock music remains the most popular music for most Americans.

Rocky Mountains

The Rocky Mountains form one of the world's great mountain systems. They stretch for 3,000 miles (4,800 kilometers), from Alaska to New Mexico. They separate the Great Plains on the east from the plateaus and mountains to the west. (*See* **Pacific Mountain System.**)

The Rockies form the continental divide of North America. East of the divide, streams and rivers flow toward the Arctic Ocean or the Mississippi River. West of it, they flow into the Pacific Ocean. (*See* **continental divide.**)

The Rockies begin with the Brooks Range, north of the Arctic Circle. The Brooks Range runs east-west through northern Alaska. Then the Rockies curve southeastward through Canada's Yukon Territory and Northwest Territories, where they form the Mackenzie and Selwyn ranges. They continue south through the Canadian provinces of British Columbia and Alberta. The highest peak in the Canadian Rockies is Mount Robson in British Columbia, which is 12,972 feet (3,954 meters) tall.

In the United States, the Rocky Mountains divide into many ranges. In Montana and Idaho, the belt of ranges is almost 400 miles (640 kilometers) wide. The Rockies' highest peaks are all in Colorado. More than 50 peaks rise over 14,000 feet (4,200 meters) above sea level. The tallest is Mount Elbert, at 14,433 feet (4,330 meters). The Colorado Rockies are so high that some of their valleys are 1 mile (1.6 kilometers) above sea level!

The Rockies extend south from Colorado and Utah into New Mexico and Arizona. The portion of the same mountain system in Mexico is the Sierra Madre Oriental.

Traveling through the Rockies would be very difficult except for the many *passes* —low places between the mountains. Indians showed the passes to white explorers. Then trappers showed settlers where their wagons could get through. Now railroads and highways use the passes. In Colorado, there are few passes, so tunnels have been blasted through the mountains.

Hikers near the top of a peak in Colorado's Rocky Mountain National Park.

History Millions of years ago, the area was under a sea. Layer upon layer of mud, sand, and shells collected and formed *sedimentary rock*. Then pressure within the earth's crust forced the rock upward. The layers of rock arched, crumpled, and fell across each other, and the Rocky Mountains were born. In some places, hot melted rock from deep within the earth formed lava flows and volcanoes. (*See* **Yellowstone National Park.**)

Wind and water—running and frozen—wore away the new landscape for millions more years. On many of the highest peaks, erosion bared the ancient granite and other rocks that used to lie beneath the sedimentary rocks. Over time, the granite peaks were eroded, too. Deep valleys were cut, and many major rivers were formed.

Then, about a million years ago, *glaciers*—huge ice sheets—formed. As they moved downhill, they wore away the mountains even more. The peaks became more pointed, and the valleys became deeper and steeper. These forces of nature combined to produce spectacular scenery.

Many Indian tribes have lived in the Rockies. The first Europeans in the area were Spanish explorers and missionaries who came north from Mexico in the late 1500s. In the middle of the 1700s, French explorers named the region *Montagnes des Roches,* which means "Rocky Mountains."

The first non-Indian to cross the Rockies was Alexander Mackenzie—a Scotsman from Canada. He went through the Canadian Rockies and traveled to the Pacific Ocean in 1793. In 1805, the American explorers Meriwether Lewis and William Clark crossed the Rockies through what are now the states of Montana and Idaho. (*See* **Lewis and Clark Expedition.**)

Zebulon Pike and other explorers called the Rocky Mountain region a desert where crops would not grow. Little rain falls in many parts of the Rockies, yet there is plenty of moisture on the high slopes, in the valleys, and in the northern forests.

The Rocky Mountains' natural resources have brought many people to the region. Between the 1820s and the 1840s, Canadian and American traders came for the fur of beavers and other animals. Many of them were also explorers and guides. They showed settlers how to get to Oregon and California.

Precious metals were discovered in the Rockies beginning in 1859. Mining towns sprang up. Billions of dollars' worth of gold, silver, copper, lead, zinc, uranium, and other minerals have been mined there.

The mountains' wide ranges and green valleys are excellent places for raising cattle. Ranchers began keeping herds in the Rockies in the 1870s.

Today, the wilderness itself attracts people to the Rockies. They come to enjoy the scenery, to fish the mountain streams, or to ski the snowy slopes. Many of the most popular national parks in the United States and Canada are in the Rocky Mountains. (*See* **national park.**)

Some snow and ice in the high Rockies never melts, even in midsummer.